10 Minute Guide to
Memory Management

Jennifer Flynn

Revised by Robert Mullen

alpha
books

A Division of Prentice Hall Computer Publishing
11711 North College Avenue, Carmel, Indiana 46032 USA

© **1993 by Alpha Books**

Second Edition

First Printing

International Standard Book Number: 1-56761-235-0
Library of Congress Catalog Card Number: 93-71144

96 95 94 93   8 7 6 5 4 3 2 1

Interpretation of the printing code: the rightmost number of the first series of numbers is the year of the book's printing; the rightmost number of the second series of numbers is the number of the book's printing. For example, a printing code of 93-1 shows that the first printing of the book occurred in 1993.

Screen reproductions in this book were created by means of the program Collage Plus from Inner Media, Inc., Hollis, NH.

Printed in the United States of America

Publisher: *Marie Butler-Knight*
Associate Publisher: *Lisa A. Bucki*
Managing Editor: *Elizabeth Keaffaber*
Acquisitions Manager: *Stephen Poland*
Development Editor: *Faithe Wempen*
Manuscript Editor: *Audra Gable*
Cover Designer: *Dan Armstrong*
Designer: *Amy Peppler-Adams*
Indexers: *Jeanne Clark*
Production Team: *Diana Bigham, Tim Cox, Mark Enochs, Joe Ramon, Carrie Roth, Barbara Webster*

Special thanks to Mike Hanks for ensuring the technical accuracy of this book.

Contents

Introduction

It's looking like a horrible day. When you try to start one of your favorite programs, you keep getting an Insufficient memory message. What does this stupid message mean, and how do you fix it? The most frustrating part is that you know you're not stupid—all you need is someone to tell you in plain English (and not in some kind of high-tech computerese) how to solve the problem so you can get on with your life. So what do you do?

A few things are certain:

- You need a quick and easy method to determine what the problem is.

- You need to understand the tasks necessary to accomplish your particular memory goals.

- You need a clear-cut, plain-English guide that explains memory management in layperson's terms.

You need the *10 Minute Guide to Memory Management*.

Why Bother with Memory Management?

There are many reasons why you should get involved with managing the memory on your PC. By streamlining your memory usage, you can benefit by:

- Having a faster, more efficient PC.

- Resolving "out of memory" problems.

- Utilizing all of your computer's memory—not just the small part that DOS accesses.

To achieve these results, you need to understand a bit about memory and how it works. That's where the *10 Minute Guide to Memory Management* comes in.

Why DOS Can't Solve Your Memory Problems for You

DOS is your PC's *Disk Operating System.* DOS handles the overall functions of your computer, such as reading a disk or saving a file. DOS also manages the use of memory.

Memory (which you will learn more about in Lesson 1) is an area in your computer where information is placed temporarily while it's being worked on. The memory area of your PC can be thought of as a desktop, where papers get shuffled, words get changed, and calculations get resolved. Memory is your PC's most precious resource, and unfortunately, DOS does a pretty bad job of managing it.

Long ago, the creators of DOS divided the memory area of your PC into two sections: the area that DOS needs for itself, and the area that your programs use. Unfortunately, today's complex, memory-hungry programs find it difficult to live in the tiny space allotted to them so long ago by the creators of DOS. Equally unfortunate, DOS itself depends on these arbitrary limitations in order to work correctly, so there is little that can be done to improve DOS.

The techniques you learn in this book will enable you to overcome the limitations of DOS and to manage memory efficiently.

What This Book Teaches

This book teaches you only *what you need to know* in order to manage your computer's memory. You can learn how to:

- Identify and solve memory problems.

- Provide the right type of memory for your programs.

- Access the current memory limitations in your PC, and "break the barriers."

- Make instant improvements with easy techniques.

- Force DOS to manage memory as efficiently as possible.

- Improve memory handling with step-by-step strategies, written for your type of PC.

In addition, there are several memory maps located on the inside covers of this book that show how your computer's memory is used.

Conventions Used in This Book

Each of the short lessons in this book include step-by-step instructions for performing specific tasks. The following special icons are included as a means of helping you quickly identify particular types of information:

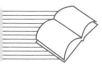

Plain English   icons appear wherever a new term is defined. Watch for this symbol to help you learn the terms you'll need to understand how memory works.

Panic Button   icons appear next to areas where new users might run into trouble. Watch for this symbol to help you avoid making mistakes.

Timesaver Tip   icons offer shortcuts and hints on how to use the ideas presented most effectively. Watch for this symbol to identify ways to save time when configuring memory on your PC.

In addition to the above icons, the following conventions are also used:

`Text you type`	Information you must type appears in bold, color, monospace font.
Keys you press	Keys you must press or items you must select appear in color.
`On-screen text`	Messages that are displayed on-screen appear in a special monospace font.

Selection letters   Selection letters for selecting menu items and commands appear in bold. In this book, the boldface letter corresponds to the underlined letter you see on-screen. Use these keys to select items with the keyboard instead of the mouse.

Key combinations   In many cases, you are instructed to press a two-key combination in order to enter a command (for example, "press Alt+X"). In such cases, hold down the first key and press the second key.

For Further Reference . . .

If you decide, after completing this book, that you want a more detailed guide to understanding memory management, I suggest that you check out these two books:

Memory Management for All of Us by John M. Goodman, Ph.D.

Windows Resource and Memory Management by Robert Mullen.

Acknowledgments

Thanks to the great editorial and production staff at Alpha Books for turning this manuscript into a good-looking book. Thanks to Bob Mullen for revising the book in its second edition, and to Mike Hanks for ensuring technical accuracy.

Trademarks

All terms mentioned in this book that are known to be trademarks or service marks are listed below. In addition, terms suspected of being trademarks or service marks have been appropriately capitalized. Alpha Books cannot attest to the accuracy of this information. Use of a term in this book should not be regarded as affecting the validity of any trademark or service mark.

Lesson 1
A Place to Begin: An Introduction to Memory

In this lesson, you will learn about the different types of memory.

Taking a Quick Tour Inside Your Computer

Your computer is made up of many parts—a keyboard, a monitor, and a system unit (the box that the monitor sits on). Inside the system unit are the components that make up the heart of your PC, as Figure 1.1 shows.

- **System board** Known also as the *motherboard*, it acts as a giant circuit board that connects the various electronic pieces of your PC.

- **Central Processing Unit (CPU)** This microchip is the brain of your computer. The CPU type is indicated by a small number, such as 80386 or 80486, imprinted on the top of the microchip. The speed at which a CPU processes information is rated in megahertz (MHz), such as 25 Mhz or 33 MHz.

1

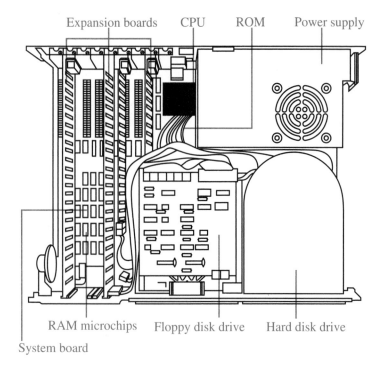

Expansion boards   CPU   ROM   Power supply

RAM microchips   Floppy disk drive   Hard disk drive

System board

Figure 1.1   A look inside a system unit reveals a computer's most important parts.

• **Memory**   Memory is composed of microchips. The two types of memory are RAM and ROM, which you will learn about later in this lesson.

• **Hard drive**   Known also as hard disk. This is the C or D drive where you store programs and data files.

• **Expansion boards**   Optional circuit boards that expand the capability of your computer, such as by adding additional memory.

- **Floppy drive**   A floppy drive reads removable diskettes that you place in its slot. Like the hard drive, diskettes store data, although in smaller amounts.

- **Power supply**   This unit powers and cools your computer.

What Is Memory?

Memory is a location inside your PC where information is stored on microchips. Your computer has many types of memory that store information in different ways and for different lengths of time.

Memory   *Memory* is a location inside your PC where information is stored on microchips.

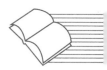

Why Isn't Disk Storage
the Same as Memory?

A disk (hard or floppy) is a storage area too, but not a microchip-based one. Disks contain a magnetic film on which information is stored via tiny magnetic particles. Most microchips store information through a pulse of electricity that is either on or off. (You will learn how information is stored in a Lesson 2, "RAM and What You Should Know About It.")

Disks are used primarily to store information on a permanent basis. Memory, in contrast, is used primarily as a workspace and as a temporary storage area.

The Different Types of Computer Memory

Your PC uses two basic types of memory, *Random Access Memory (RAM)* and *Read Only Memory (ROM)*.

RAM is comprised of tiny electronic microchips that hold a charge of electricity. The pattern formed by these charges represents the data stored there. ROM is a single microchip that has had its electronic information permanently "burnt-in" to the circuitry inside the microchip.

Reading information from RAM and ROM is much faster than reading information from a disk, because the information stored there is completely electronic and involves no moving parts.

ROM or Read Only Memory

ROM can be read, but not written to. That's why it's called *Read Only Memory*. Information contained in ROM is permanent, and it cannot be changed.

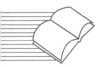 **ROM** *ROM* contains permanent information about the basic operations of your computer.

ROM contains permanent information that is basic to every computer, such as a startup program which checks the computer's parts before starting the operating system. Another important program stored in ROM is the Basic Input/Output System or BIOS, which controls how information is retrieved or transferred to the monitor, keyboard, disk drives, RAM, and ROM.

RAM or Random Access Memory

RAM can be both read and written to. The information stored in RAM can be read randomly, in any order (hence the name, *Random Access Memory*). Your computer uses RAM like a desktop, as a place to temporarily store information on which it is working. Because data can be read randomly from RAM, it doesn't matter which specific memory location is used to store that data, as long as the CPU can find it.

RAM *RAM* provides temporary storage of information, creating the working area of your computer. Information is calculated, changed, and otherwise manipulated in RAM.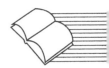

When the computer is turned off, information in RAM is erased (the desktop is cleared). You must make sure that you transfer your data from RAM to disk storage before turning off the computer. The act of transferring data from RAM to disk is called *saving a file*. It is also a good idea to save your data periodically while you are working, in case of a power outage.

Other Uses for RAM

Besides your main system, other types of RAM can be found in other areas of your computer, including:

- A *cache*   A place created in RAM where the most often used data is stored for faster access. The advantages and disadvantages of creating RAM caches are discussed in Lesson 18, "Caching in on a Good Thing."

- A *printer buffer*   A place where printer data is held until the printer can print it. Printer buffers let a PC turn over printer data and then continue working as the printer continues to print.

- *Video RAM*   Allows complex video graphics to be displayed quickly on your computer's monitor. Video RAM acts in a manner similar to a printer buffer.

- *Shadow RAM*   Makes your PC run faster by copying information from ROM into RAM. When basic input or output instructions are needed, those instructions are read from RAM, which is faster than trying to read them from ROM.

- *CMOS RAM* (or Complimentary Metal-Oxide Semiconductor)   Semipermanent RAM. The CMOS RAM in your PC keeps basic information about your computer, such as the amount of memory, the type of monitor, and the size and type of each drive. CMOS RAM also maintains your PC's internal clock. Unlike regular RAM (which provides only temporary storage), the information stored in CMOS RAM is kept "permanent" by a battery that provides a constant charge to the CMOS microchip. However, when the battery goes out, the data is lost and must be reloaded or restored from a backup.

Now that you have learned a little about memory, let's take a closer look at RAM and how it is divided.

Lesson 2
RAM and What You Should Know About It

In this lesson, you will learn how your computer uses memory. You will also learn how memory is divided by DOS.

How Memory Adds Up

RAM is made up of bits and bytes. A *bit* (**B**inary Dig**it**) is a single electronic charge, either positive or negative (*on* or *off*). A *byte* is a group of 8 bits which represents a character, such as the letter A or the number 101. You rarely hear memory discussed in terms of bits or bytes, but *kilobytes* and *megabytes* instead.

Bits and Bytes   One byte is made up of 8 bits. One Kilobyte (1K) is about 1,000 bytes (really it's 1,024 bytes). One Megabyte (1MB) is 1,024K, or about 1,000,000 bytes (really it's 1,048,576 bytes). Confusing? Yes it is, but if you think of 1K as 1 thousand, and 1MB as 1 million, you'll be pretty close.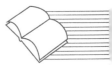

How Your Computer Uses RAM

As you've learned in the Introduction and Lesson 1, the memory area of your PC can be thought of as a desktop. A program places information on this desktop in order to change it, calculate it, or otherwise manipulate it. Because of the limitations of DOS, the size of the desktop (the memory dedicated to program use) is relatively small.

When you start a program under DOS, the program grabs as much program memory as it needs. During program execution, it may request more memory, and as long as memory is available, the program gets it. If additional memory is not available, the program may stop running, or may issue some kind of error message (such as `Insufficient memory`).

As you create documents, the data you type is kept in RAM; if you create large documents, your program requires large amounts of RAM to manipulate the information in the document. By learning how to manage memory, you can provide additional memory to your programs.

When you exit a program, the memory it used is freed (erased) to make room for the next program you run. All information on the desktop (RAM) will be lost, unless you copy it to your hard disk or a floppy diskette before you exit your program.

DOS and the 640K Limit

DOS, along with ROM BIOS (Basic Input/Output System) organizes files, handles data retrieval, and manages memory.

DOS manages the first megabyte of RAM. That 1MB is divided into two sections: one section for DOS's own use, and the other section for use as a workspace for programs, as Figure 2.1 shows.

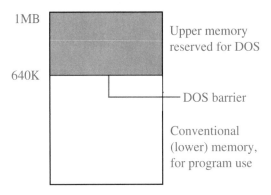

Figure 2.1 DOS divides the first megabyte of RAM into two sections.

DOS's original designers never dreamed that a program would need more than 640K of memory, so they didn't plan for it. As a result, DOS is not designed to allow programs more than 640K of "desktop space." This arbitrary division of the 1MB of RAM available to DOS has become known as the 640K barrier, or simply the *DOS barrier*, because it limits the amount of space that your programs can run in.

DOS Barrier The division between conventional (lower) memory, which is the area of memory from 0K to 640K, and upper (system) memory, which extends from 640K to 1MB. This barrier separates the section of memory that programs use from the area reserved for DOS.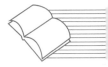

The top part of DOS's memory area is called *upper* or *system memory*, and as mentioned earlier, it was designed for DOS's own use. The bottom part of DOS's memory area is called *conventional* or *lower memory*, and it is available for your programs. (Some computers have more than 1MB of memory—which DOS cannot access, but other programs can. That additional memory also has a name, as you'll learn in the following sections.)

Conventional Memory   The area of memory below 640K. This is the area of memory that your programs run in.

Ready for more bad news? Not all of that limited 640K of conventional memory is actually available for use by programs. When your PC starts (a process called *booting*), DOS is copied from the hard drive (or a diskette in drive A) into conventional memory. When I say that DOS is copied into memory, I mean that the command processor, COMMAND.COM (which interprets simple DOS commands like COPY and DIR), is copied into RAM, along with the DOS BIOS routines. These DOS BIOS routines act in conjunction with the ROM BIOS that you read about in Lesson 1 to implement input and output. In a nutshell, you could say that when you turn on your PC, DOS sets up shop in RAM.

After the basic DOS routines are loaded, DOS stakes out an area in conventional memory for keeping track of open files. This area is called the system data area. Next, device drivers are copied into conventional memory.

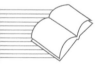

Device Drivers   *Device drivers* are special programs that augment DOS's capability to support the PC's hardware. For example, if your PC has a mouse, it also has a device driver file that tells the CPU how to send and receive signals from it.

In addition, any specific configuration requests (from CONFIG.SYS) are also loaded. What you typically have left for programs to use after DOS is loaded is anywhere from 620K to 420K, depending on the DOS version. In Lessons 12 and 15, you will learn how to move DOS out of conventional memory, giving your programs more room to run.

After you load DOS, you might see a picture of memory that looks something like Figure 2.2.

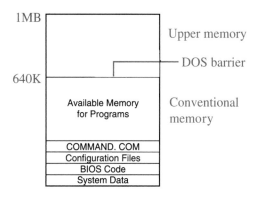

Figure 2.2   It sure is getting crowded in here.

Now that you understand what the DOS barrier is, let's learn how to bust it.

Lesson 3

Ways to Break the DOS Barrier

In this lesson, you will learn how to overcome the DOS barrier with other types of memory.

Conventional memory is very precious because it's the main memory that your programs use. Conventional memory is the only area of memory in which a program can run, but a program can sometimes use other areas of memory to store data as it works. In this lesson, we will explore how your programs can access other areas of memory.

Upper Memory

The area above conventional memory is called *upper memory*. Upper memory falls between 640K and 1MB. This area, like conventional memory, can be directly accessed by DOS, but it is not available for your programs to use. It is considered "reserved."

Upper Memory   The area of memory between 640K and 1MB.

Upper memory was envisioned as the area where DOS would store its BIOS, or Basic Input/Output System, as Figure 3.1 shows. The BIOS, you may recall, controls how devices, such as disk drives and monitors, are accessed by the computer. Some types of ROM use this area, such as the ROM chips which control your hard disk and your monitor. There is also an area in upper memory which is called video RAM; images are placed here before they are displayed on your monitor.

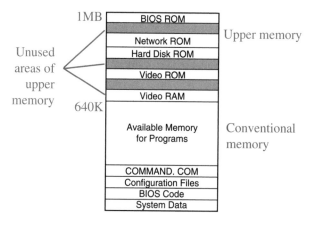

Figure 3.1   Upper memory is reserved for DOS.

Many areas of upper memory go unused. These unused areas are called *UMBs*, or *Upper Memory Blocks*. By using an upper memory device driver, you can utilize these seldom-used areas of upper memory. For example, these unused areas can be filled with memory that can be used for loading device drivers and TSRs (terminate and stay resident programs) that would otherwise take up some of your conventional memory.

TSRs   TSRs are special utility programs that load into memory and "go to sleep" until you activate them with a special key combination. TSRs are background programs (such as a calculator or a notepad) that can be used while you're working in another program.

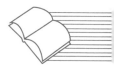

13

To make these UMBs available for use, you must have DOS 5 or 6, or some type of memory management program. (DOS 5 and 6 require at least a 386 microprocessor, or CPU, to make UMBs available.) You will learn how to utilize UMBs in later lessons.

Extended Memory

Extended Memory (*XMS* or *Extended Memory Specification*) is the memory above the 1MB mark. If your PC has a total of 4MB of RAM, 3MB of that memory is extended memory. In order to use extended memory, your PC must have at least a 286 CPU and a special device driver file called an *extended memory manager*. Our map of memory now looks like the one in Figure 3.2.

Extended Memory   The area of memory above 1MB.

The CPU cannot access extended memory in its normal operating mode, which is called *real mode*. In real mode, the CPU can manage only the memory addresses up to the 1MB mark.

Real mode is labeled as such because the memory addresses that DOS uses are the actual memory addresses being used by the CPU. Imagine that DOS is the post office. DOS has a fixed number of mailboxes, and each mailbox represents a section of memory from 0K to 1MB. Everything in real mode works out great for DOS, because there is a mailbox for every part of memory that can be accessed (from 0K to 1MB).

In order to address memory areas above 1MB, the CPU must be switched to another mode which is called *protected mode*. In protected mode, the CPU can create additional addresses for memory above 1MB.

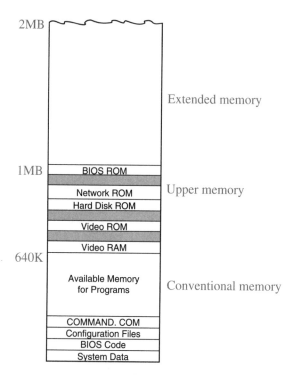

Figure 3.2 Our vision of memory is extended into the area past 1MB.

These additional addresses are accessed by going behind DOS's back (remember that DOS can't deal with memory addresses above 1MB) with the help of the extended memory manager. It's as if the post office delivered a letter to an address in Queens (which is within the post office's territory), but the recipient in Queens hand-delivered the letter to the Bronx (without the post office knowing about it).

Programs must be written to specifically use extended memory—that is, they have to know how to use the extended memory manager to go behind DOS's back. Some popular programs that use extended memory include Windows, DESQview, Lotus 1-2-3 version 3.x, and AutoCAD. For programs that use expanded memory (explained later in this lesson), extended memory can be made to simulate expanded memory. You will learn how to change extended memory into expanded memory in later lessons.

High Memory Area

The first 64K of extended memory is called the *high memory area,* or *HMA.* This area is available on PCs with a 286 microprocessor (and above). DOS can access this area directly, with the help of an HMA (High Memory Area) device driver.

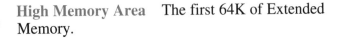

High Memory Area   The first 64K of Extended Memory.

A high memory device driver enables you to move DOS, device drivers, and TSRs out of conventional memory, although the HMA is usually used to move just DOS. Upper Memory Blocks are usually used for device drivers and TSRs.

Expanded Memory

Expanded memory (*EMS* or *Expanded Memory Specification*) is another kind of RAM. Like extended memory, it cannot be used for running programs, but only for temporarily storing program data. However, unlike extended memory, expanded memory can be reached by DOS *directly*, with the help of an expanded memory device driver.

Extended memory is not accessed through DOS, but through an extended memory manager that reroutes requests for memory (behind DOS' back) to memory addresses above 1MB. Expanded memory, on the other hand, can be accessed by DOS through a window located in upper memory. So now our memory map looks like Figure 3.3.

Expanded Memory Special memory that is linked to the rest of the system through a window in upper memory. Extended memory can sometimes be made to simulate expanded memory.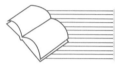

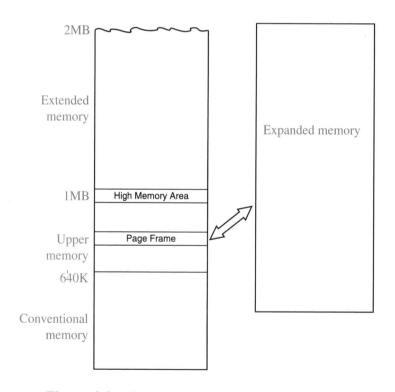

Figure 3.3   Our view of memory has expanded.

The gateway to expanded memory lies in an unused area of upper memory called a *page frame*. The page frame is a 64K area created by the expanded memory device driver. The page frame acts as a sort of Ellis Island, with data being copied from expanded memory into the page frame for processing, and then back out again.

By using a special driver, you can make extended memory simulate expanded memory (for instance, if you want to run a program that requires expanded memory).

In the next lesson, you will learn how to determine your system's memory.

Lesson 4
How Much Memory Does Your System Have?

In this lesson, you will learn how to determine the amount of memory your PC has by using the MEM command.

Using the MEM Command

The MEM command can be used to display your PC's memory configuration. To use MEM, follow these steps:

1. Type MEM.

2. Press Enter.

Bad command or filename If you get this error message, change to the DOS directory (type CD\DOS) and then try again.

The MEM command in DOS 6 is a little different from that of DOS 5, so let's look at each individually.

If You Are Using DOS 5 . . .

When you use the MEM command with DOS 5, you see
something like this:

```
655360     bytes total conventional memory
655360     bytes available to MS-DOS
510512     largest executable program size
3145728    bytes total contiguous extended
           ➥memory
3145728    bytes available contiguous
           ➥extended memory
```

This section lists the amount of conventional memory
available. This PC has 655,360 bytes or 640K of conventional memory (remember that 1K is equal to 1,024 bytes).
DOS is being loaded into conventional memory, so there
are only 510,512 bytes (about 499K) of conventional
memory left available.

The second section of two lines shows us the amount of
extended memory. Extended memory is memory located
about the 1MB mark. This particular computer has 314,728
bytes or about 3MB of extended memory. Information
regarding the area of memory between 640K and 1MB is
not available with the MEM command if you're using DOS
version 5.0.

May I See a Program?   With DOS 5, you can
include a /P or /PROGRAM switch at the end of the
MEM command—for example, MEM /P. This lists
all the programs that are in memory. With DOS 6,
however, the /P switch does something totally different—it makes the display show one "page"
(screenful) at a time.

20

If You Are Using DOS 6 . . .

When you use the MEM command with DOS 6, you see
something like this:

```
Memory Type          Total =  Used  +  Free
_____             ___      ___       ___

Conventional         640K     100K      540K
Upper                187K      28K      159K
Adapter RAM/ROM      197K     197K       0K
Extended (XMS)      7168K    2488K     4680K
_____             ___      ___       ___

Total memory        8192K    2813K     5379K


Total under 1 MB     827K     128K      699K


Largest executable program size   540K (552544
                                    ➡ bytes)
Largest free upper memory block    0K  (162736
                                    ➡ bytes)
MS-DOS is resident in the high memory area.
```

The first line of detail lists the amount of *Conventional*
memory available, used and free. This PC has 655,360
bytes or 640K of conventional memory. (Remember that
1K is equal to 1,024 bytes.) The DOS system files and some
TSR's are being loaded into conventional memory, so
there's only 552,544 bytes (about 540K) of conventional
memory free.

The second line of detail shows you the amount of
Total, Used and Free *Upper* memory. Remember that
Upper memory is the amount of memory located above
640K and below 1MB. This particular PC has 159K free,

because we haven't loaded any TSR's and device drivers there yet.

The third line of detail shows you the amount of *Adapter RAM/ROM* memory. *Adapter RAM/ROM* memory is the portion of memory where instructions for your computer's hardware devices are kept while the computer is powered-up. *Adapter RAM/ROM* memory is *also* located in the region of memory starting at 640K and extending to 1MB. This PC has about 197K of *Adapter RAM/ROM* memory in total, and all of it is in use (none is *Free*).

The fourth line of detail shows us how much *Extended (XMS)* memory is enabled *Total*, *Used*, and *Free*. Extended memory is defined as being a memory that is located above 1,024K. This particular computer has 7,168K of extended memory, and 2,488K of it is in use.

Using the MEM /CLASSIFY Switch

With both DOS 5 and DOS 6, you can use the /C switch to get more detailed information about how memory is being used.

1. Type MEM /CLASSIFY or simply MEM /C.

2. Press Enter.

MEM /C with DOS 5 . . .

In DOS 5, you'll see see something like this:

```
Conventional Memory :
Name               Size in Decimal    Size in Hex
------             ------------------  ------------

MSDOS              73520      ( 71.8K)    11F30
NAV_               37184      ( 36.3K)    9140
ANSI                4192      (  4.1K)    1060
MOUSE              17280      ( 16.9K)    4380
SHARE               6192      (  6.0K)    1830
COMMAND             4704      (  4.6K)    1260
SAVE               72624      ( 70.9K)    11BB0
FREE                 176      (  0.2K)    B0
FREE                  64      (  0.1K)    40
FREE              438128      (427.9K)    6AF70


Total  FREE :     438368      (428.1K)


Total bytes
available
to programs:      438368      (428.1K)
Largest
executable
program size:     437856      (427.6K)
```

3145728 bytes total contiguous extended memory
3145728 bytes available contiguous extended memory

  The first column lists the program's name. The next
column lists the size of the program in bytes and kilobytes.
The last column lists the program's size in hexadecimal, a
special numbering system that your computer uses for its
internal functions.

It Scrolls By Too Fast!   In DOS 5, if your MEM
command fills more than one screen, you can show
one screen at a time by adding I MORE to the end of
the command—for example, MEM /C I MORE.

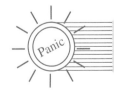

23

MEM /C with DOS 6 . . .

If you're using DOS 6, MEM /C produces more detailed results:

```
Modules using memory below 1 MB:

Name        Total   =   Conventional   +   Upper Memory
————        —————       ————————           ————————

MSDOS       13661      (13K)   13661   (13K)   0        (0K)
SETVER      576        (1K)    576     (1K)    0        (0K)
HIMEM       1152       (1K)    1152    (1K)    0        (0K)
EMM386      3125       (3K)    3120    (3K)    0        (0K)
ANSI        4208       (4K)    4208    (4K)    0        (0K)
DBLSPACE    44384      (43K)   44384   (43K)   0        (0K)
COMMAND     2960       (3K)    2960    (3K)    0        (0K)
AD-DOS      5940       (5K)    5040    (5K)    0        (0K)
DOSKEY      4144       (4K)    4144    (4K)    0        (0K)
SHARE       6208       (6K)    6208    (6K)    0        (0K)
MOUSE       17088      (17K)   17088   (17K)   0        (0K)
SMARTDRV    28800      (28K)   0       (0K)    28800    (28K)
Free        715440     (699K)  552656  (540K)  162784   (159K)
```

```
Memory Summary:

Type of Memory   Total      =   Used          +   Free
————————         ——————         ——————            ——————

Conventional     655360  (640K)   102704  (100K)    552656  (540K)
Upper            191584  (187K)   28800   (28K)     162784  (159K)
Adapter RAM/ROM  201632  (197K)   201632  (197K)    0       (0K)
Extended (XMS)   7340032 (7168K)  2547712 (2488K)   4792329 (4680K)

Total memory     8388608 (8192K)  2880848 (2813K)   5507760 (5379K)

Total under 1 MB 846944  (827K)   131504  (128K)    715440  (699K)
```

```
Largest executable program size      552544     (540K)
Largest free upper memory block      162736     (159K)
MS-DOS is resident in the high memory area.
```

The *Modules using memory below 1 MB:* section is a list of the programs in your computer's memory. This section specifies where each loaded program resides in your computer's memory, a major improvement over the DOS 5 MEM /C report.

It Scrolls By Too Fast! In DOS 6, to see one screen at a time, you can use the DOS 5 trick of adding | MORE to the end of the command, or you can use the /P switch. I know, I know, in DOS 5 the /P switch was something different, but in DOS 6, /P means "one page at a time." Your command line would look like this: MEM /C /P.

What's MEM Good For?

The results of the MEM command change as you reconfigure your PC to take advantage of the techniques in this book. Feel free to use either the MEM or the MEM /C commands as you work to verify your current memory situation. For example, you could use the MEM /C command to quickly verify which device drivers and TSR's have been moved successfully out of conventional memory.

25

Other Memory Detection Software

Finding out how your system uses memory is critical in managing memory effectively. Although the MEM command does not tell you much about your system, it is a place to begin. There are many commercial software packages that you can buy to help you do more effective detective work. Some of these software packages are designed for DOS, while others work with a popular operating environment, Windows. It is interesting to note that most of these programs come bundled with a complete memory management package. Table 4.1 shows a list of some popular memory detection software.

Table 4.1   Popular memory detection software.

Software name	Company	Works with	Notations
ASQ	Qualitas	DOS	Bundled with 386MAX
Control Room	Borland Int'l	DOS	
InfoSpotter	RenaSonce Group	DOS	
Manifest	Quarterdeck	DOS	Bundled with QEMM-386
WinSleuth Professional	Dariana	Windows	
Skylight	RenaSonce Group	Windows	

In this lesson, you learned how to access your system's memory usage. In the next lesson, you will learn how a special file called CONFIG.SYS can effect memory usage.

Lesson 5
Easy Ways to Check Memory

In this lesson, you will learn other ways (besides the MEM command) to determine how much memory your PC has.

A Memory Test at Startup

When your PC *boots* (starts), it goes through a self check called *POST* or *Power On Self Test*. This test checks your PC's equipment and each RAM chip. As each RAM chip is tested, the total RAM checked is displayed on the monitor. By watching the monitor during the POST, you can determine how much RAM you have.

You may have to *reboot* (restart) your computer several times before you are able to read all of the information that POST displays. If you see only one number displayed on your monitor (in the upper left corner of the screen), this number is the total amount of RAM. On some computers, you may see two numbers; the number on the left represents the amount of conventional memory, the number on the right represents the amount of extended memory.

Hold Your Horses! If the POST test encounters any problems as it tests each RAM chip, your computer may stop (lock up). Some type of error message appears, along with a number which helps to identify the errant chip.

What Your System Displays After the POST Test

After the POST test is complete, your PC may load special memory device drivers in order to make upper memory, high memory, extended memory, or expanded memory ready to use. You'll see the contents of your AUTOEXEC.BAT file scroll across your screen as its commands are processed one by one. Some programs may report their status when they load. Eventually, you'll come to the end of the startup files, and you'll see the DOS prompt.

Displaying Available Memory with CHKDSK

CHKDSK is a DOS command that you can run with either DOS 5 or DOS 6 which shows available memory. However, unlike MEM, CHKDSK is available under *all* DOS versions, not just versions 5 and 6.

Follow these steps to issue the CHKDSK command:

1. Exit any program you may be using. If your program has an option that lets you go to DOS, do not use it; exit the program instead.

2. At the DOS prompt, type c: and press Enter.

3. Type CHKDSK.

When you use the CHKDSK command, you see something like this:

```
Volume HARDDISK C created 07-22-1992 9:45a
Volume Serial Number is 186A-BC9A
168132608 bytes total disk space
   163840 bytes in 6 hidden files
   708608 bytes in 167 directories
156540928 bytes in 4452 user files
 10702848 bytes available on disk
     4096 bytes in each allocation unit
    41048 total allocation units on disk
     2613 available allocation units on disk
   655360 total bytes memory
   510512 bytes free
```

CHKDSK does not reveal as much as MEM does about the type and amount of memory that your PC has; it tells you more about your hard disk. However, if you look at the last set of numbers, you see that this system has 655,360 total bytes memory. If you remember that one kilobyte is equal to 1,024 bytes, then you can convert this number to 640K.

The next message you see tells you that there are only 510,512 bytes free. DOS may be using some of conventional memory, leaving a smaller amount available. You will learn how to move DOS and other utilities out of conventional memory, leaving more memory for your programs.

I Thought My PC Had More Memory! Even if your PC has more than 640K RAM, CHKDSK won't report it. You need to run MEM to see any RAM above the 640K mark.

What Are Lost Chains, and How Do I Fix Them?

When you run CHKDSK, you may see a message such as:

```
Errors found, F parameter not specified
Corrections will not be written to disk

2 lost allocation units found in 1 chains.
8192 bytes disk space would be freed.
```

This message indicates that your hard disk has some lost allocation units (lost clusters). This is caused when DOS does not update its file listing when manipulating files. The file listing indicates that a file exists, but the data cannot be tracked to any particular file.

Lost clusters will probably not cause a memory problem, but they may make your hard disk think it's out of space or cause other glitches. To get rid of lost clusters, type:

```
CHKDSK /F
```

When prompted, answer Y for yes. The /F parameter tells CHKDSK to correct the file listing. The data that was in the lost cluster is given a file name such as FILE0001.CHK. Use the DEL command to delete these files and free up the space.

What's a CONFIG.SYS and Why Do I Need One?

In this lesson, you will learn about the CONFIG.SYS file.

What Does the CONFIG.SYS Do?

The *CONFIG.SYS* file is used to customize DOS. The CONFIG.SYS can load special device drivers for optional PC equipment, such as a mouse, or for software, such as a virus detection program. The CONFIG.SYS can change DOS system parameters, such as FILES, BUFFERS, and so on. You will learn more about these system parameters in this lesson.

Where the CONFIG.SYS File Must Be Located

The CONFIG.SYS file does not exist until you create it, using some type of text editor. The CONFIG.SYS file must be placed in the root directory of your *boot drive* (the drive which is accessed at startup), which is usually drive C.

When you boot (start) your computer, DOS checks for the presence of the CONFIG.SYS file. The specified device drivers are loaded into RAM, and system parameters are changed as requested. If no CONFIG.SYS file exists, the default values for the system parameters are used.

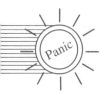

Remember to Reboot! The CONFIG.SYS is read only at boot time; if you make changes to the CONFIG.SYS, you must reboot (restart) your computer to make those changes effective.

Looking Inside Your CONFIG.SYS

A CONFIG.SYS file can have different statements in it; some are must-haves, some are not. Before I discuss some of the more common ones, you may want to print a copy of your existing CONFIG.SYS for reference.

To print a copy of your CONFIG.SYS, verify that your printer is ready and then type

```
PRINT C:\CONFIG.SYS
```

When you press Enter, you may see a message asking you which list device (printer) to use. In most cases you can simply press Enter and your CONFIG.SYS will be printed.

If you don't want a printed copy of your CONFIG.SYS, you can use the TYPE command to view the contents:

```
TYPE CONFIG.SYS
```

Figure 6.1 shows the results of this command.

```
C:\>type config.sys
DEVICE=C:\WINDOWS\HIMEM.SYS
DOS=HIGH,UMB
DEVICE=C:\WINDOWS\EMM386.EXE NOEMS
DEVICEHIGH=C:\BIN\NAV\NAV_.SYS
DEVICEHIGH=C:\DOS\ANSI.SYS
DEVICEHIGH=C:\WINDOWS\MOUSE.SYS
FILES=28
BUFFERS=30
SHELL=C:\DOS\COMMAND.COM /P /E:256
BREAK=ON


C:\>
```

Figure 6.1   You can verify the contents of your
CONFIG.SYS file with the TYPE command.

Want to Make a Change?   If you want to make
any of the changes to your CONFIG.SYS discussed
in this chapter, read Lesson 10 or 13 for instructions
on how to use the MS-DOS or DR DOS editor.

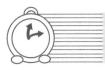

Device Drivers

Device drivers are special programs that supplement the
BIOS. DOS's BIOS (which is automatically loaded) includes support for standard equipment such as a hard disk
or floppy diskette drive. Optional device drivers, called
installable device drivers, are loaded through the
CONFIG.SYS and include mouse, tape drive backup system, or network interface drivers.

33

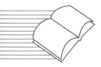 **Installable Device Drivers** Installable device drivers are programs that supplement the DOS BIOS system. These drivers provide instructions to DOS on how to interface with various optional hardware.

To specify a device driver in your CONFIG.SYS, follow this syntax:

```
DEVICE=drive:\directory\devicedrivername
```

Substitute the actual drive, directory, and device driver file name for the words in italics.

For example, I have a mouse on my PC, so my CONFIG.SYS includes the following:

```
DEVICE=C:\MOUSE.SYS
```

MOUSE.SYS is the name of my particular mouse device driver. I keep it on drive C, in the root directory (C:\). It doesn't matter what directory you use to store individual device drivers, as long as you include the directory name in the CONFIG.SYS file.

 **A Rose by Any Other Name** Most device drivers end in .SYS, so they are usually easy to identify. You may already be using a common device driver, ANSI.SYS, to enhance monitor and keyboard control.

 **Rocky Mountain High** You will learn in later lessons about two commands, DEVICEHIGH (for MS-DOS 5) and HIDEVICE (for DR DOS). These commands can be used to load device drivers into upper memory.

The BUFFERS Statement

The *BUFFERS* statement sets the number of *disk buffers*. Disk buffers increase the speed of your computer. Disk buffers create a *cache* in RAM, containing information recently read from disk. When a request for data occurs, a quick scan of the disk buffer is made. If the requested data is in the disk buffer, then the data is transferred from the buffer into the program's working area in RAM. Because the transfer is between two areas of RAM, this process is very fast. A typical BUFFERS statement looks like this:

```
BUFFERS=20
```

Disk Buffers   An area in RAM that stores recently read data that is scanned prior to transferring data from the hard drive.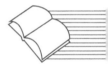

You might think that using more buffers always improves program performance, but it's not that simple. When a data request comes in, DOS must search the entire buffer area for a match. If no match is found, DOS has wasted time. Also, each buffer decreases the amount of conventional memory available to your programs (unless you use extended or expanded memory for your buffers, which will be discussed in later lessons).

Programs typically specify the number of buffers that they require for peak performance. A complex database program may require 20 or even 30 buffers; a word processor, probably requires only 10 to 15. If you're using SMARTDRV or another disk cache program, you can set your buffer statement really low; you will learn more about disk caches in Lesson 18, "Caching in on a Good Thing." Juggle the numbers of all of your programs to arrive at the best compromise.

The FCBS Statement

FCBS stands for *File Control Block System*, which is an area in RAM that stores information about open files. File control blocks are a bit outdated; older programs used them to keep track of open files, but new programs use file handles for the same purpose. If several files need to be opened at the same time, the FCBS area must be large enough to track each file.

It is unlikely that you need the FCBS statement in your CONFIG.SYS. The default value is 4 file control blocks, which use 40 to 60 bytes each. *If you are not attached to a network,* you might want to consider setting FCBS to 1 by typing this command:

```
FCBS=1
```

The FILES Statement

The *FILES* statement is similar to FCBS, and is also used to track open files. Each file handle uses from 40 to 60 bytes of RAM. Most programs specify the number of file handles that they need. Set your FILES statement to the highest of those numbers, such as

```
FILES=20
```

The default for FILES is 8, which is always too small, so you should set FILES to some number that is higher. Twenty is usually a good number, but certain multitasking environments, such as Windows and GeoWorks, require around 30.

Get a Handle on It The FILES area can be moved into upper memory by DR DOS and some memory management programs, such as QEMM-386. You'll learn more about this in upcoming lessons.

The STACKS Statement

The *STACKS* statement is used to keep track of *interrupts.* Interrupts are sent by the computer's various hardware components (keyboard, disk drive, mouse, and so on) to get the CPU's attention. For example, when you press a key or click a mouse button, you create an interrupt—that is, you interrupt whatever the CPU was doing, to tell it to do something else.

Interrupts *Interrupts* are a means for some hardware component (such as a keyboard or a mouse) to get the CPU's attention.

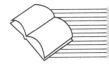

When an interrupt occurs, the CPU stops what it is doing to attend to it. The CPU uses the stack area (an area in RAM) to hold what it was working on, so that after the CPU handles the interrupt, it can get back to it. Think of this process as "making a quick note" so that the current action is not forgotten or lost.

Problems occur because interrupts can be interrupted, too. In other words, while the CPU is handling one interrupt, it can get *another* interrupt call, preventing it from returning to its original task. In this manner, interrupt requests get *nested,* and when the CPU has handled each interrupt, it eventually makes its way up the stack to its original task. If the stack area is not big enough to record all of the interrupts that occur (but have not yet been handled by the CPU), an error message appears:

```
Internal Stack Failure, System Halted
```

If this happens frequently, you can use the STACKS statement to increase the default number of stacks. The syntax for the STACKS statement is:

```
STACKS=numberofstacks,sizeofstacks
```

For example:

```
STACKS=9,128
```

The default number of stacks varies by machine, but it is frequently set to STACKS=9,128, which creates a stack area of nine stacks of 128 bytes each. This default of STACKS=9,128 (which is valid for an 80286 or higher CPU) uses a little over 1K of RAM. You rarely need to increase the STACKS statement, because most programs today create their own private stacks in memory when they need them. You may even want to set the general stack area to zero to save RAM:

```
STACKS=0,0
```

The SHELL Statement

During the boot process, the DOS command interpreter, COMMAND.COM, is loaded into RAM. The *SHELL* statement lets you specify where COMMAND.COM is located on your boot disk, or use a third-party command interpreter instead of COMMAND.COM.

Another reason for using the SHELL statement (and one that affects RAM), is the capability of the SHELL statement to increase the *environment space*. You may recall from Lesson 4 that the environment is a notation area where both DOS and program variables are placed. The value of these variables affects DOS or program behavior.

Environment Space   A notation area in RAM where both DOS and program variables are placed.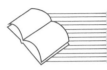

If you use many environment variables such as PATH or SET, you may run out of room in the environment area. To increase the environment area, you can use the SHELL statement. The syntax for the SHELL statement is:

```
SHELL=drive:\directory\commandinterpeter \P
\E:environmentspace
```

For example, to increase the environment area from its default of 160 bytes to 256, use this statement:

```
SHELL=C:\COMMAND.COM \P \E:256
```

You need to increase the environment area if you see the message Out of environment space.

Be Careful Using the SHELL Statement!   Because the SHELL statement loads the DOS command interpreter, if it is not typed in properly, it can literally cripple your computer. Follow the instructions in the next lesson to create a boot diskette before you attempt to make any changes to your CONFIG.SYS, especially changes involving the SHELL statement.

In this lesson, you learned about the CONFIG.SYS. In the next lesson, you will learn how another file, the AUTOEXEC.BAT, also affects memory.

What's an AUTOEXEC.BAT and How Does It Affect Memory?

In this lesson, you will learn about the special file, AUTOEXEC.BAT, and how it affects memory.

What Is an AUTOEXEC.BAT?

An *AUTOEXEC.BAT* is a special file that automatically executes commands when you start your system. You can use the AUTOEXEC.BAT to make changes to the DOS environment or to start programs.

Like the CONFIG.SYS file, the AUTOEXEC.BAT is created using a text editor and is placed in the root directory of the boot drive.

Some commands that are typically found in an AUTOEXEC.BAT file use RAM, which is why you must be concerned about them. Before I discuss some of the more common ones, you may want to print a copy of your existing AUTOEXEC.BAT for reference.

To print a copy of your AUTOEXEC.BAT, verify that your printer is ready and then type:

40 `PRINT C:\AUTOEXEC.BAT`

When you press Enter, you may see a message asking you which list device (printer) to use. In most cases you can simply press Enter and your AUTOEXEC.BAT will be printed.

If you don't want a printed copy of your AUTOEXEC.BAT, you can use the TYPE command to view the contents:

```
TYPE AUTOEXEC.BAT
```

Figure 7.1 shows the results of this command.

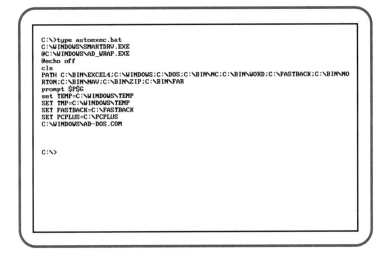

```
C:\>type autoexec.bat
C:\WINDOWS\SMARTDRU.EXE
@C:\WINDOWS\AD_WRAP.EXE
@echo off
cls
PATH C:\BIN\EXCEL4;C:\WINDOWS;C:\DOS;C:\BIN\NC;C:\BIN\WORD;C:\FASTBACK;C:\BIN\NO
RTON;C:\BIN\NAV;C:\BIN\ZIP;C:\BIN\FAR
prompt $P$G
set TEMP=C:\WINDOWS\TEMP
SET TMP=C:\WINDOWS\TEMP
SET FASTBACK=C:\FASTBACK
SET PCPLUS=C:\PCPLUS
C:\WINDOWS\AD-DOS.COM


C:\>
```

Figure 7.1   You can verify the contents of your AUTOEXEC.BAT with the TYPE command.

Want to Make a Change?   If you want to make any of the changes to your AUTOEXEC.BAT discussed in this chapter, read Lesson 10 or 13 for instructions on how to use the MS-DOS or DR DOS editor.

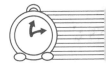

The PATH Statement

The *PATH* statement provides DOS with a list of directories to search for program files not located in the current directory. As you may recall from Lesson 4, the contents of the PATH statement are copied into the DOS environment space, which is a note-keeping area of RAM.

A typical PATH statement looks like this:

```
PATH=C:\WINDOWS;C:\DOS;C:\NC;C:\WORD;C:\FASTBACK;
C:\NORTON;C:\NAV;C:\ZIP;C:\FAR
```

Each directory in the PATH statement is separated by a semi-colon. When you use long PATH statements like this one, the environment area becomes full, and may have to be enlarged. The environment area can be made bigger through the SHELL statement (see Lesson 6). When you make the environment area bigger, you use more RAM.

Environmentally Smart If you look at the output of the MEM /P command shown in Lesson 4, you notice items listed as Environment. These are copies of the environment area that are given to each program as it starts. Keeping the environment area small reduces the total amount of RAM used by the multiple copies of the environment space.

Other Ways the AUTOEXEC.BAT Uses RAM

Certain commands placed in the AUTOEXEC.BAT also use RAM:

- *RAM cache* speeds the access to files by keeping the most often requested files in memory. RAM caches are sometimes created through commands in the CONFIG.SYS, but be careful: DOS 5's new SMARTDRV.EXE file is loaded through the AUTOEXEC.BAT. You will learn more about RAM caches in Lesson 18.

- The *PROMPT* command is used to customize the DOS prompt. A common variation of the PROMPT command is PROMPT PG. The contents of the PROMPT command are stored in the environment area (and use RAM), just like SET and PATH.

- You can load special programs called *TSRs* (*terminate and stay resident*). These utility programs go to sleep after they start, and they are reactivated when you want them by a special key combination. You use TSRs with other programs. One popular TSR, SideKick, provides a notepad, a calculator, an appointment scheduler, and an address book. For example, you could activate SideKick while you are in your word processor to add a column of figures or change an appointment.

  Each TSR uses RAM. With both DOS 5 and DOS 6, you can load TSRs into upper memory and out of conventional memory.

Lesson 8

Creating an Emergency Diskette

In this lesson, you will learn how to create an emergency diskette called a *boot diskette*.

Why Do I Need a Boot Diskette?

A *boot diskette* is a diskette you can use to start your PC, if you have trouble booting your PC from the hard drive. Having a boot diskette is always a good idea, but it becomes especially important whenever you plan to edit your PC's CONFIG.SYS file, as you'll be doing in later lessons.

If you're using DOS 5, and a problem with your CONFIG.SYS or AUTOEXEC.BAT keeps you from running your computer, you will need to use a Clean Boot diskette. If you're using DOS 6, you can use two new features to avoid having to reboot your computer with a Clean Boot diskette in a floppy drive.

Murphy's Law?   Many things can prevent your system from booting. Create a boot diskette following the instructions included in this lesson and keep it in a safe place.

44

If You're Using DOS 6

If you're using DOS 6, you get to use some new features that can help you out of a bad situation when you've edited your CONFIG.SYS or AUTOEXEC.BAT files incorrectly. There are two new features of DOS 6 called Clean Start and Interactive Start. These two startup features can help you solve your problems during the boot sequence without the use of a special Clean Boot diskette.

When you boot your computer (with DOS 6 installed) you see a statement on your display that reads Starting MS-DOS.... When you see this message, you can press one of two F-keys to invoke either the Clean Start or the Interactive Start process.

Clean Start

Clean Start allows you to reboot your system without loading the CONFIG.SYS and AUTOEXEC.BAT files at all. If you've made a change to your CONFIG.SYS file and your system locks-up or acts unpredictably, you can press the F5 key when you see the message Starting MS-DOS... to go right to your C: prompt.

None of the files named in your CONFIG.SYS and AUTOEXEC.BAT files will be loaded because Clean Start treats your CONFIG.SYS and AUTOEXEC.BAT files as though they don't exist. You can then run your text editor program to find and correct any problems arising from entries made in either of these files. With this new feature of DOS 6, you don't have to have a clean boot diskette just because of entries made in the CONFIG.SYS and AUTOEXEC.BAT files.

Interactive Start

Interactive Start allows you to review and run or skip each line in your CONFIG.SYS file. Interactive Start lets you run every line in your CONFIG.SYS file individually. You approve or disapprove of the running of each line as it comes up for execution. Interactive Start asks you if you want to run each line in turn. If you know which line is causing problems, you can run the rest of the CONFIG.SYS file and omit the execution of just the one problematic line.

Interactive Start will help a lot if you're using Stacker or SuperStor because you might have to run the lines that enable these compressed drives in order to use a text editor located on one of those compressed drives.

Here's how Interactive Start works:

1. You reboot your machine as you would normally.

2. When you see the statement Starting MS-DOS..., press the F8 key.

3. The first line in your CONFIG.SYS file will be displayed along with a prompt to execute the line or skip the line.

4. Interactive Start accepts your input, then goes on to the next line in your CONFIG.SYS file until all of the lines are reviewed by you.

If you see a line during the boot process that you suspect to be the culprit of a problem, you tell Interactive Start not to run that particular line. Then you run the rest of your CONFIG.SYS file line-by-line. You can correct a problem related to an entry with a text editor without having to reboot the machine from a Clean Boot floppy disk.

Interactive Start *doesn't* step its way though your
AUTOEXEC.BAT file, so if your problems lie there, you'd
best use Clean Start (F5) to get to your text editor in order
to fix the problem.

What Makes a Good Boot Diskette

Let's say you don't have DOS 6, or for some reason want
to use a boot diskette anyway. Read this section to learn
about boot diskettes.

When your PC boots, it checks drive A first. If there's
a disk there, the PC boots from it. If not, the PC boots from
the hard disk. Therefore, you must have your boot diskette
in drive A. Here are the files needed for the boot diskette:

- The DOS operating system files (COMMAND.COM
  plus two hidden files)

- A copy of your PC's CONFIG.SYS file

- A copy of your PC's AUTOEXEC.BAT file

- One copy of each of the programs and device drivers
  listed in your CONFIG.SYS and AUOTEXEC.BAT
  files

- A copy of your PC's CMOS information

Step One: Copying the
DOS Operating System Files

To copy the operating system files onto a diskette, you need
to format that diskette with a special FORMAT command.

Formatting   The process of preparing a diskette for use.

Follow these steps to format a diskette and copy the operating system files. Remember that you must use drive A, because if your hard drive won't boot, drive A is used to start your system.

1. Turn on your PC, and insert a diskette into drive A. (Make sure the diskette does not contain any data that you will need later. Any data on the diskette will be erased during this process.)

2. Type CD\DOS and press Enter to change to the DOS directory.

3. Type FORMAT A:/S and press Enter. This formats the diskette and copies the three operating system files.

Giving It the Boot   Placing the operating system files onto any diskette makes it *bootable*, which means that the diskette can be used to start your PC.

Step Two: Copying CONFIG.SYS

Now that you have a formatted, bootable diskette, you need to add additional configuration files to make the diskette usable for emergencies. The first of these files is the CONFIG.SYS.

Follow these steps to add the CONFIG.SYS file:

1. Make sure that the bootable diskette from step one is still in drive A.

2. Type COPY C:\CONFIG.SYS A: and press Enter. This copies the CONFIG.SYS file onto the diskette in drive A.

3. Copy any special driver files that CONFIG.SYS uses. For example, if your CONFIG.SYS uses a disk driver called C:\DRIVER.SYS, you would type the following to copy the file:

```
COPY C:\DRIVER.SYS A:
```

4. Repeat this command to copy all of the necessary driver files.

Step Three: Copying AUTOEXEC.BAT

After you have copied your CONFIG.SYS file, copy the AUTOEXEC.BAT file onto your bootable diskette. Follow these instructions to copy your AUTOEXEC.BAT:

1. Make sure that the bootable diskette from step two is still in drive A.

2. Type COPY C:\AUTOEXEC.BAT A: and press Enter. This copies the AUTOEXEC.BAT file onto the diskette in drive A.

3. Copy any special driver files that the AUTOEXEC.BAT uses. For example, if your AUTOEXEC.BAT uses a disk driver called C:\DRIVER.SYS, you would type the following to copy the file:

```
COPY C:\DRIVER.SYS A:
```

4. Repeat this command to copy all of the necessary driver files.

Step Four: Copying Your CMOS Data

If your PC has a special chip (called a CMOS chip) which retains basic configuration data for your PC, it is very important that you make a copy of it.

Hopefully, your PC comes with a utility for reading the CMOS chip and making a copy of it. If not, there are many utilities which are available at no charge on local bulletin board systems (BBS). These utilities include: CMOSSAVE & CMOSRSTR, CMOSPUT & CMOSGET, and CMOS.EXE. Some popular disk utilities, such as Norton Utilities, also provide this capability. Use these utilities to save your CMOS data on your boot diskette. Figure 8.1 shows CMOS information as seen in Manifest, QEMM-386's memory management tool. You will learn more about Manifest in Lesson 22.

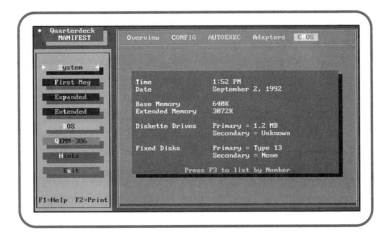

Figure 8.1 CMOS RAM stores important configuration information.

Seeing It in Print   Until you can purchase a utility that lets you copy your CMOS data onto your boot diskette, you can protect yourself by printing a copy of the data. When your system boots, it will probably display some message indicating which key to press to enter CMOS Setup. Press this key and, with your printer turned on, use the Print Screen key (or the Shift+Print Screen combination) to print a copy of each screen in the CMOS setup.

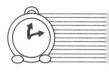

Protecting Your Boot Diskette

Once you have created a boot diskette, make sure that you *write-protect* it. To write-protect a 5 1/4-inch diskette, place a write-protect tab (it looks like a small piece of black or silver tape) over the notch on one side of the diskette.

To write-protect a 3 1/2-inch diskette, push the small tab located in one corner of the diskette towards the diskette's edge. When the tab is set for write-protect, you can see through the hole where the tab is located.

If you make changes to your CONFIG.SYS or AUTOEXEC.BAT, be sure to copy the new versions of those files (after testing them) onto your boot diskette. In order to copy files onto your boot diskette, you will need to temporarily remove the write-protection by reversing the process described earlier. After updating your boot diskette, remember to restore the write-protection!

The Ultimate Test   After you have created your boot diskette, test it! Place your diskette in drive A and boot your system. If you do not get a DOS prompt A:, there is something wrong with your

diskette, and you may need to edit your configuration files. You will learn how to edit your configuration files in Lessons 10 and 13.

Keeping Your Boot Diskette Current

Prior to installing any new software, upgrading DOS, or attempting to edit the CONFIG.SYS or AUTOEXEC.BAT files, update your boot diskette with current copies of your configuration files. That way, if anything goes wrong, you will have safe copies of your configuration files to go back to.

After you have thoroughly tested the new versions of your CONFIG.SYS or AUTOEXEC.BAT, you can repeat these steps to make your boot diskette current. Use the following simple steps to update your boot diskette. (If your boot drive is not C, substitute that drive's letter for C in these commands.)

1. Place your boot diskette in drive A.

2. Type COPY C:\CONFIG.SYS A: and press Enter.

3. Type COPY C:\AUTOEXEC.BAT A: and press Enter.

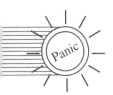

Before You Copy   Always test your configuration files after editing them but before you save them to your boot diskette (to make sure that you like them and want to keep them). That way, only usuable copies of your configuration files will be saved on your boot diskette.

Lesson 9
How DOS Can Improve Your System's Memory

In this lesson, you will learn about the DOS 5 and DOS 6 memory management commands, what they do, and how they can be used to configure memory.

Why Are DOS 5 and 6 Different from Older Versions?

New commands included in DOS 5 and 6 put you more in control of how memory is used on your PC. With these two latest versions of DOS, your PC will have the capability to:

- Load DOS into the high memory area, freeing valuable conventional memory.

- Load TSRs and device drivers into upper memory, also freeing conventional memory.

- Simulate expanded memory with extended memory (memory above the 1MB mark).

- Make extended memory available to programs which use it.

This lesson summarizes how these features work. Later lessons will explain in detail how to use each one to maximize your computer's memory.

Is There a DR in Your House? If you use DR DOS, you have the same capabilities listed above. Read the rest of this lesson to learn how these memory commands work, then skip to Lessons 14 and 15 to learn the specifics of each command.

Accessing the High Memory Area

The *high memory area* (or *HMA*) is found in the first 64K of extended memory (see Figure 9.1). The HMA is accessible only on PCs with a 286 microprocessor (and above). With the help of the high memory device driver, you can move DOS, device drivers, and TSRs into the high memory area and out of conventional memory. That device driver is called HIMEM.SYS in MS-DOS, HIDOS.SYS for 286 PCs in DR DOS, and EMM386.SYS for 386 and above in DR DOS.

If You Use Windows and HIMEM.SYS A copy of HIMEM.SYS comes with Windows, so compare the dates on both files (with the DIR command) before you decide which HIMEM.SYS file to use. Always use the most current version of HIMEM.SYS.

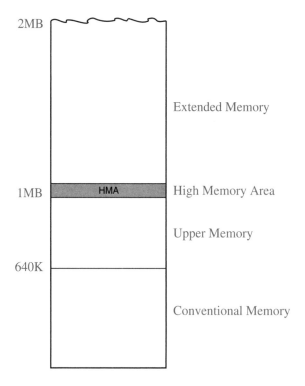

Figure 9.1 The HMA is located in the first 64K of extended memory.

Loading DOS into the High Memory Area

Both DOS 5 and 6 allow you to load a portion of DOS into the HMA. Once the high memory area is available, DOS can be moved into the HMA and out of conventional memory. The benefit of loading DOS into high memory is obvious; conventional memory (which would otherwise be

used by DOS) is freed and made available for your programs to use. In DOS 5 and 6, the command DOS=HIGH
is used (after the HIMEM.SYS driver is loaded) to move
DOS and DOS data structures into the high memory area
(see Figure 9.2).

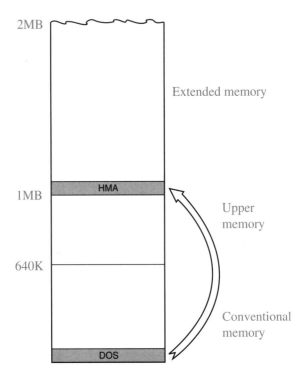

Figure 9.2   Moving DOS into high memory frees
conventional memory space.

DR DOS works a bit differently. By loading HIDOS.SYS
or EMM386.SYS, DOS itself is loaded into high memory
automatically. In DR DOS, the command HIDOS=ON is
used (after the HIDOS.SYS or EMM386.SYS driver is
loaded) to move the rest of DOS (the DOS data structures,
such as buffers) into the high memory area.

Loading Device Drivers and TSRs into Upper Memory

Both DOS 5 and DOS 6 give you the capability of placing both device drivers and TSRs in upper memory. Upper memory is the memory area between 640K and 1MB. Upper memory is an area used by BIOS ROM and some types of ROM chips, such as those which control your hard disk and your monitor. Many areas of upper memory go unused. These areas are called *upper memory blocks* or UMBs. Through the use of an upper memory device driver, you can utilize this seldom used area of memory (see Figure 9.3).

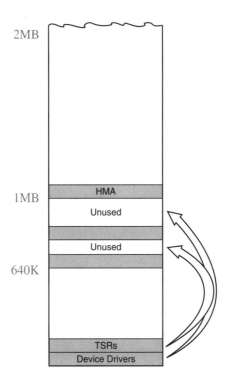

Figure 9.3 Device drivers and TSRs can be loaded into upper memory.

57

These UMBs can be mapped to expanded memory using DOS by a three-part process:

1. Load HIMEM.SYS (the driver that provides access to the high memory area).

2. Load EMM386.EXE (the driver that controls expanded memory).

3. Use the DOS=UMB command (which transfers the command of the expanded memory areas in upper memory to DOS).

After you have created UMBs, you can use the DOS commands LOADHIGH (for loading TSRs) and DEVICEHIGH (for loading devices).

DR DOS lets you load device drivers and TSRs in a similar manner. The two-part process used in DR DOS to create UMBs includes:

1. Loading either EMM386.SYS or HIDOS.SYS (drivers that provide access to the high memory area and upper memory and that control expanded memory).

2. Using HIDOS=ON.

After you create UMBs, you can use the DR DOS commands HIINSTALL (for loading TSRs) and HIDEVICE (for loading devices). Another command, HILOAD, can be used to load TSRs into upper memory from AUTOEXEC.BAT, instead of from CONFIG.SYS.

Making Extended Memory Available

Extended memory is the area of RAM above the 1MB mark. Extended memory can be used for data storage by programs that are designed for it. To make extended memory available under both DOS 5 and 6, you load the EMM386.EXE device driver.

DR DOS uses either HIDOS.SYS or EMM386.SYS to make extended memory available.

Creating Expanded Memory with Extended Memory

Extended memory can be made to simulate expanded memory. The gateway to expanded memory lies in an unused area of upper memory called a *page frame*. The page frame acts as a sort of Ellis Island, or processing station, with data being copied from expanded memory into the page frame for processing and then back out again.

With DOS 5 and 6, there are two steps in the process of simulating expanded memory: loading HIMEM.SYS (to provide access to the high memory area) and loading EMM386.EXE (to create the page frame in upper memory and to control expanded memory).

Expanded memory is created through a page frame (whose start address you can specify) in upper memory. Four pages of 16K each are created within the page frame,

59

and these pages are used to swap memory back and forth between the pages in upper memory and extended memory. Why do you need to swap data into upper memory? Because DOS can't directly access memory above 1MB, but it can access upper memory.

DR DOS uses one driver to simulate expanded memory, the EMM386.SYS. Another driver, EMMXMA.SYS, is used on IBM PS/2 computers with special expanded memory boards to access expanded memory.

In this lesson, you learned how DOS versions 5 and 6 make it possible for you to improve memory management on your PC. In the next lesson, you will learn how to use the editor program that comes with both DOS 5 and 6 to implement memory management commands. If you use DR DOS, you may want to skip the next three lessons (which cover the MS-DOS memory management commands) and go directly to Lesson 13, where you will learn how to use the DR DOS editor.

Lesson 10

Editing Your Configuration Files with MS-DOS

In this lesson, you will learn how to edit your CONFIG.SYS and AUTOEXEC.BAT files using the editor that comes with DOS 5 and DOS 6.

A Word Before You Use EDIT

In Lessons 6 and 7, you learned some CONFIG.SYS and AUTOEXEC.BAT basics. Now you're ready to learn to edit those files. This lesson shows you the mechanics of editing with EDIT, the text editor that comes with DOS 5 and DOS 6. In later lessons, you'll learn the exact changes to make. When you edit your configuration files, keep these things in mind:

- Don't edit CONFIG.SYS or AUTOEXEC.BAT without backing-up these two files on your boot diskette. Instructions on making a boot diskette are covered in Lesson 8.

- The order of the statements within a configuration file is sometimes important. Later lessons will address this in more detail.

- Make sure you keep the appropriate number of files and buffers in your CONFIG.SYS. (Refer to Lesson 6 for details.)

- After making changes to a configuration file, make sure you reboot your PC to make those changes effective.

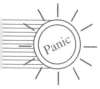

Copy Cat! It is a good practice to make a copy of your original file before you start editing. Follow the procedures outlined in Lesson 8 to create a boot diskette to keep current copies of your CONFIG.SYS and AUTOEXEC.BAT files. Always test your edited files before you save them on your boot diskette.

Getting Down to BASICs In order to use the text editor that comes with both DOS 5 and 6, you will need the QBASIC files that are placed in your DOS directory during installation. Don't delete the QBASIC files to make room for other things; you'll render the editor inoperable.

Using EDIT

EDIT is an easy-to-use, full-screen text editor that comes with DOS 5 and DOS 6. Although it's beyond the scope of this book to teach you everything you might need to know about using EDIT, this lesson will teach you enough to edit simple files such as CONFIG.SYS and AUTOEXEC.BAT.

You Don't Have DOS 5 or DOS 6? If you have a prior version of DOS, you can use EDLIN instead of EDIT. Read the instructions in your DOS manual to learn how to use EDLIN.

Do I Really Need EDIT? To edit simply text files like CONFIG.SYS and AUTOEXEC.BAT, you need an editor capable of saving in text mode. Most word processors can do this. If you have a word processor that you feel comfortable using, read the instruction manual to determine if it can save files in text mode.

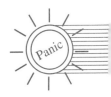

Starting EDIT

Follow these steps to start EDIT:

1. Type EDIT.

2. Press Enter. The EDIT opening screen appears (see Figure 10.1).

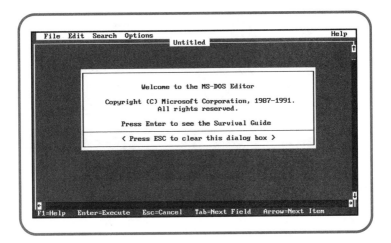

Figure 10.1   The EDIT opening screen.

63

Opening a File to Edit

Now that you have the editor started, you need to open a file to work on. When using the editor, you can use the keyboard or click (press the left mouse button while pointing) to issue commands. Follow these steps:

1. Press Alt+F. (Press the Alt key, hold it down, press F and then release.) If you have a mouse, you can click on the File menu item to open the File menu.

2. Press O or click on the Open command.

3. Type the name of the file you want to edit and press Enter. For example, you could type `c:\CONFIG.SYS`. The file you requested is opened, as Figure 10.2 shows.

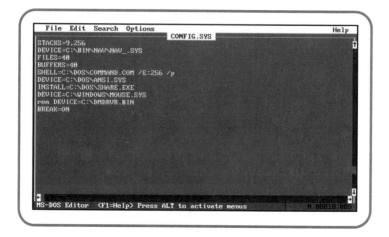

Figure 10.2 The CONFIG.SYS file is ready to edit.

Making Changes

Once a file is open, you can make changes to it. Although there are many ways to move around the screen, the most commonly used methods are these:

To move:	Press:
Up, down, left, or right	Arrow keys
To the beginning of a line	Home key
To the end of a line	End key
To the beginning of the next line	Ctrl+Enter
To the top of the window	Ctrl+Q, then E
To the bottom of the window	Ctrl+Q, thenX

When you start EDIT, you are in the *insert mode*. That means when you position your cursor and start to type, the text you type is inserted at that point, and all existing text is pushed to the right. If you want to type over existing characters, press the Insert key. You are now in *overtype mode*.

If you want to delete some characters, position your cursor on any character and press the Delete key.

Saving Your File

After making changes to your file, you must save it before exiting the editor. To save your changes:

1. Press Alt+F or click on the File menu to open it.

2. Press S or click on the Save command.

3. If you want to keep your original file intact (without changes) and save this file under a new name, press A or click on the Save As command. Type the new file name and press Enter.

Exiting EDIT

After you have saved your changes, you can safely exit the editor.

1. Press Alt+F or click on the File menu to open it.

2. Press X or click on the Exit command.

 **Made a Mistake?** If you decide, after making changes to a file, that you do not want to save those changes, simply exit the editor without saving.

In this lesson, you learned how to use the text editor that comes with DOS versions 5 and 6. In the next lesson, you will learn how to use some of the DOS 5 and DOS 6 memory management commands.

Lesson 11

Managing Conventional Memory with MS-DOS

In this lesson, you will learn how to use HIMEM.SYS and EMM386.EXE, the DOS 5 and DOS 6 memory management commands.

In earlier chapters, you've learned about the PC configuration files and how to edit them. You've also learned about memory and how DOS versions 5 and 6 can help you manage it. Now you're ready to roll up your sleeves and learn exactly how to take advantage of your new knowledge.

Know Your Options Some commands have many variations. In this lesson and the next, you will learn only the options for each command that are commonly used. Consult your DOS manual if you're interested in the advanced options.

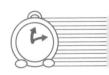

I'm Scared! Tinkering with your PC's memory usage is not as hard as it sounds, but if you're truly scared, jump to Lesson 22 and try DOS 6's MemMaker or one of the third-party products described there.

Understanding the Syntax for Commands

Interpreting the syntax for commands is easy when you know how. Take this fictitious command:

```
DEVICE=[drive:\directory\]FAKEDEVICE [mode] [ON¦OFF]
```

Words in CAPITAL LETTERS should be typed exactly as shown.

Words in *italics* should be replaced with the real name involved. For example, you would not type the word *directory*, but the actual name of the directory involved.

Words in [brackets] are optional; do not use these options unless you need them.

Words separated with ¦ present an either/or situation. For example, the [ON¦OFF] command is in brackets because it is optional, but if you use it, you would use either the ON or the OFF option.

Using HIMEM.SYS

The device driver, *HIMEM.SYS*, is used in the CONFIG.SYS to provide access to the high memory area. The command that loads the HIMEM.SYS driver *should be first* within the CONFIG.SYS. However, if your system loads a device driver that provides access to your hard drive, that command should be placed first, *just before* the HIMEM.SYS command. Also, if you are using any memory management software, make sure you load HIMEM.SYS *before* any memory management command.

HIMEM.SYS Syntax

The syntax for loading the HIMEM.SYS driver is:

```
DEVICE=[drive:\directory\]HIMEM.SYS
[/MACHINE:xxxx]
[/A20CONTROL:ON¦OFF]
```

Some of the options (which appear in brackets) for loading HIMEM.SYS are:

drive:\directory The *drive* and *directory* where the HIMEM.SYS file can be found, for example, C:\DOS\HIMEM.SYS.

/MACHINE:*xxxx* *xxxx* indicates both the type of machine you have, and the type of A20 handler (used to access high memory) to use. Allowable values include (1 is the default):

Machine	xxxx Code
AT	1
PS/2	2
PT1 Cascade	3
HP Vectra	4
ATT 6300 Plus	5
Acer 1100	6
Toshiba	7
Wyse	8

/A20CONTROL:ON¦OFF Controls whether the A20 handler is "grabbed" by HIMEM.SYS, if it was already on

69

when HIMEM.SYS was loaded. If you specify *ON*, HIMEM.SYS grabs the A20 handler. If you specify *OFF*, HIMEM.SYS does not grab the A20 handler unless it is off.

HIMEM.SYS has several advanced options that can be used to specify:

- The minimum number of kilobytes a program must request before being allowed to use high memory.

- The number of extended memory block handles that can be used at one time.

- The amount of memory allocated to the 15H interrupt interface. (Applications can use the 15H interrupt to access extended memory.)

- Whether shadow RAM is enabled.

- Whether a great deal of information is displayed on your screen when HIMEM.SYS is loaded and run.

Use DOS's manual or on-line help if you're interested in any of these advanced options.

HIMEM.SYS Examples

The simplest way to load HIMEM is by typing the command:

```
DEVICE=C:\DOS\HIMEM.SYS
```

If you get a message indicating that HIMEM was Unable to control A20 line, then you must tell HIMEM what type of PC you have with the \MACHINE:*xxxx* command. If your PC is not one of the ones listed, use the TYPE

command to read the README.TXT file in your DOS
directory, or check the owner's manual. To specify a
Toshiba, type:

```
DEVICE=C:\DOS\HIMEM.SYS /MACHINE:7
```

If you get a message indicating that The A20 line was
already enabled, then use the /A20CONTROL:ON switch:

```
DEVICE=C:\DOS\HIMEM.SYS /A20CONTROL:ON
```

Remember to Reboot After making any changes
to your CONFIG.SYS, make sure you reboot your
computer to have those changes take effect.

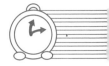

If you're using DOS 5, you'll see this message when
HIMEM.SYS is loaded:

```
HIMEM: DOS XMS Driver, Version 3.07-02/14/92
Extended Memory Specification (XMS) Version 3.0
Copyright 1988-1992 Microsoft Corp.

Installed A20 handler number 14.
High Memory Area is available.
```

If you're using DOS 6, you won't see any message
when HIMEM.SYS is loaded unless you use this command
line switch in your CONFIG.SYS file:

```
DEVICE=HIMEM.SYS /V
```

The /V command line switch stands for "verbose."
When you specify the /V switch with DOS 6, you see a
message similar to the default one displayed by DOS 5.
If you're using DOS 6 and you need to see this message each
time you reboot your system, go ahead and include the

/V switch. Essentially, when you're using DOS 6 and you've specified the /V switch, you see the following message:

```
HIMEM: DOS XMS Driver, Version X.X
Extended Memory Specification (XMS) Version X.X
Copyright 1988-1993 Microsoft Corp.

Installed A20 handler number 1.
64k High Memory Area is available.
```

Using EMM386.EXE

The EMM386.EXE driver:

• Fills UMBs (upper memory blocks) with expanded memory so device drivers and TSRs can be loaded there.

• Provides access to extended memory for programs that use it.

• Simulates expanded memory with extended memory.

• Excludes Microsoft Windows from accessing the UMA.

EMM386 is loaded through the CONFIG.SYS file, and it must be located *after* the HIMEM.SYS command, but *before* any expanded memory commands.

EMM386.EXE Syntax

The syntax for loading the EMM386.EXE driver is:

```
DEVICE=[drive:\directory\]EMM386.EXE [mem]
[RAM¦NOEMS]
```

The options (which appear in brackets) for loading EMM386.EXE are:

drive:*directory*\   The *drive* and *directory* where EMM386.EXE can be found, for example, C:\DOS\EMM386.EXE.

mem   The number you specify with *mem* limits the amount of extended memory (in K) that simulates expanded memory. You can specify any number from 16 to 32,786. Default is 256K.

RAM or *NOEMS*   Activates upper memory blocks. If you use *RAM*, upper memory blocks and expanded memory are available. If you use *NOEMS*, upper memory blocks are available, but no expanded memory is simulated—all extended memory remains extended. If you're primarily working with Microsoft Windows programs and applications, the latter switch is the best one to use.

EMM386.EXE has several advanced options that can be used to specify:

- The exact upper memory address where the page frame starts.

- The exact upper memory address for a page.

- A range of addresses in upper memory to exclude when creating the page frame.

- The lowest address in extended memory to be used.

- The amount of extended memory (in K) that is not to be used as expanded memory.

- The number of fast alternate register sets to be used for tracking expanded memory.

- The number of page handles used.

- How much of your UMA is to be dedicated for use by Windows and not EMM386.

- Whether EMM386 is to load itself entirely into conventional memory.

- Whether you want EMM386 to exclude the use of the UMA in the event that you're getting memory error messages from your applications that reside in the UMA.

- If you want detail displayed as EMM386 is executed.

EMM386.EXE Examples

Some of these examples use the command DOS=HIGH,UMB, which is used to place DOS into high memory and to create upper memory blocks. You will learn more about the DOS=HIGH,UMB command in Lesson 12.

To create upper memory blocks and not expanded memory, use this command:

```
DEVICE=C:\DOS\HIMEM.SYS
DOS=HIGH,UMB
DEVICE=C:\DOS\EMM386.EXE NOEMS
```

Once upper memory blocks are created, you can load device drivers and TSRs into them. Extended memory, in this example, can be used by programs that are designed to use it, such as Windows.

To create upper memory blocks and 4MB of expanded memory, use:

```
DEVICE=C:\DOS\HIMEM.SYS
DOS=HIGH,UMB
DEVICE=C:\DOS\EMM386.EXE 4096 RAM
```

Don't forget to reboot after making changes. When you reboot your computer using DOS 5 and you've included the EMM386.EXE driver in your CONFIG.SYS correctly, you'll see something like this message:

```
MICROSOFT Expanded Memory Manager 386  Version X.XX
Copyright Microsoft Corporation 1986, 1991
EMM386 successfully installed.
Expanded memory services unavailable.
   Total upper memory available  . . . . . .    92 KB
   Largest Upper Memory Block available  . .    92 KB
   Upper memory starting address . . . . . .   C800 H
EMM386 Active.
```

When you reboot your computer using DOS 6 and you've included the EMM386.EXE driver in your CONFIG.SYS correctly, you'll see something like this message:

```
MICROSOFT Expanded Memory Manager 386   Version X.XX
Copyright Microsoft Corporation 1986, 1993
EMM386 successfully installed.
Expanded memory services unavailable.
   Total upper memory available  . . . . . .   155 KB
   Largest Upper Memory Block available  . .   155 KB
   Upper memory starting address . . . . . .   C800 H
EMM386 Active.
```

In this lesson, you learned the two basic DOS 5 and DOS 6 memory management commands. In the next lesson, you will learn how to load DOS, device drivers, and TSRs high, out of conventional memory into upper and high memory.

Lesson 12
Maximizing Conventional Memory with DOS

In this lesson, you'll learn how to load DOS into high memory, and you'll learn about loading device drivers and TSRs into upper memory.

DOS 6 Shortcut   If you're a DOS 6 user and are short on time or patience, you can jump to Lesson 22 and use MemMaker to maximize your conventional memory.

Using the DOS=HIGH Command

The *DOS=HIGH* command is used somewhere in the CONFIG.SYS *after* the HIMEM.SYS command, to load DOS into high memory. You can also use this command to load device drivers and TSRs into upper memory.

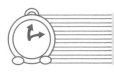

High There   Because the DOS 6 installation program adds the DOS=HIGH line to your CONFIG.SYS file if it thinks your computer will support it, the DOS=HIGH line may already be there. If so, you can skip the next section.

DOS Syntax

The syntax for using the DOS command is:

```
DOS=[HIGH¦LOW],[UMB¦NOUMB]
```

The options (which appear in brackets) for loading DOS are:

HIGH or LOW   Controls whether DOS loads into high memory. If you specify HIGH, DOS loads into high memory. If you specify LOW, DOS loads into conventional memory. Default is LOW.

UMB or NOUMB   Controls whether device drivers and TSRs load into upper memory. If you specify UMB, DOS controls the upper memory blocks and lets device drivers and TSRs load there. If you specify NOUMB, extended memory controls any UMBs created, and device drivers and TSRs are not allowed to load into upper memory. The default is NOUMB.

Up, Up, and Away!   Before you start loading device drivers and TSRs into upper memory, remember that you must load the expanded memory driver, EMM386.EXE first. Read Lesson 11 before preceding.

DOS Examples

To load DOS into the high memory area, you need two commands:

```
DEVICE=C:\DOS\HIMEM.SYS
DOS=HIGH
```

To load device drivers and TSRs into upper memory, you need several commands:

```
DEVICE=C:\DOS\HIMEM.SYS
DEVICE=C:\DOS\EMM386.EXE NOEMS
DOS=HIGH,UMB
DEVICEHIGH=device
```

Device is the name of a driver to load high. The first two commands you learned about in Lesson 11; the last one is described in the next section.

Using the DEVICEHIGH Command

The *DEVICEHIGH* command is used in the CONFIG.SYS to load device drivers into upper memory, if there is enough room for them there. If a device driver is too big to fit into upper memory, it loads into conventional memory automatically.

Necessary Partners   DEVICEHIGH won't work without HIMEM.SYS, EMM386.EXE, and DOS=HIGH,UMB.

Line Up!   Use the MEM /C command described in Lesson 4 to see which of the device drivers in conventional memory is the largest and to load them into upper memory according to size (from largest to smallest). This may require rearranging lines in CONFIG.SYS.

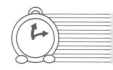

DEVICEHIGH estimates the size of a device driver and loads it into an appropriate open space in upper memory. However, some device drivers request additional memory after they have been loaded, and they can cause your system to lock up. To estimate the actual amount a device driver needs, load it into conventional memory (using the DEVICE command) and use the MEM command to view the driver's size. You can then specify the amount of memory to be assigned to a particular device driver through the SIZE option discussed in the next section.

DEVICEHIGH Syntax

The syntax for using the DEVICEHIGH command is:

```
DEVICEHIGH=[SIZE=size][drive:\directory\]driverfilename
```

The parameters for using DEVICEHIGH are:

SIZE=size Use size (in hexidecimal) to specify the minimum amount of upper memory required to load this device. A device will not be loaded if the minimum amount specified is not available. If size is not specified, DOS estimates the amount of upper memory to allocate.

drive:\directory\ The drive and directory where the device driver can be found. For example, C:\DOS\.

driverfilename The name of the driver. For example, ANSI.SYS.

DEVICEHIGH Example

To load the device driver, ANSI.SYS, into upper memory, use the following commands:

```
C:\DOS\HIMEM.SYS
DOS=HIGH,UMB
DEVICE=C:\DOS\EMM386.EXE NOEMS
DEVICEHIGH=C:\DOS\ANSI.SYS
```

Using the LOADHIGH Command

LOADHIGH is the AUTOEXEC.BAT file's equivalent of DEVICEHIGH. The LOADHIGH command is used by both DOS 5 and DOS 6 to load TSRs (and certain device drivers) into upper memory through AUTOEXEC.BAT. The same conditions for use apply as with DEVICEHIGH: HIMEM.SYS, EMM386.EXE, and DOS=HIGH,UMB must be set up first.

LOADHIGH Syntax

The syntax for using the LOADHIGH command is:

```
LOADHIGH=[drive:\directory\]driverfilename
```

The parameters for using LOADHIGH are:

drive:\directory   The drive and directory where the TSR can be found. For example, C:\DOS\.

driverfilename   The name of the driver or TSR. For example, DOSKEY.COM.

LOADHIGH Example

To load the DOS TSR, DOSKEY.COM, into upper memory,
include these commands in your CONFIG.SYS:

```
DEVICE=C:\DOS\HIMEM.SYS
DOS=HIGH,UMB
DEVICE=C:\DOS\EMM386.EXE NOEMS
```

Then include this command in your AUTOEXEC.BAT:

```
LOADHIGH=C:\DOS\DOSKEY
```

In this lesson, you learned how to load DOS, device
drivers, and TSRs into upper and high memory. The next
three lessons cover the DR DOS editor and memory management commands. You may want to skip these lessons
and continue with Lesson 16, which describes how to
maximize your system's memory.

Changing Your Configuration Files with DR DOS

In this lesson, you will learn how to edit your CONFIG.SYS and AUTOEXEC.BAT files using the DR DOS editor.

Using the DR DOS Editor

A text editor comes with DR DOS, called *EDITOR*. It is an easy-to-use, full-screen editor, similar to the DOS 5 editor. Although it is beyond the scope of this book to teach you everything you might need to know about using EDITOR, you will learn enough to edit simple files such as CONFIG.SYS and AUTOEXEC.BAT.

Before You Start Be sure to read the sections "A Word Before You Edit" and "What Are Configuration Files?" in Lesson 10 before you start editing with EDITOR.

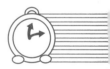

Starting the DR DOS Editor

Follow these steps to start the DR DOS Editor:

1. Type `CD\DRDOS` and press Enter to change to the DOS directory, where the editor is located.

2. Type `EDITOR` and press Enter. The EDITOR title screen appears (see Figure 13.1).

```
                      EDITOR R2.00    Full Screen Text Editor
        Copyright (c) 1988,1989,1990 Digital Research Inc. All rights reserved.



              Please enter the name of the text file you wish to edit.
              If the file does not already exist it will be created.
              Press the Esc key to leave this program.

              File name?
```

Figure 13.1 The EDITOR opening screen.

Opening a File to Edit

Now that you have the editor started, you need to open a file to work on. Follow these steps:

1. At the `File name?` prompt, type the name of the file you want to edit. For example, if you want to edit your AUTOEXEC.BAT file, type: `C:\AUTOEXEC.BAT`.

2. Press Enter, and the file is opened (see Figure 13.2).

Making Changes

Once a file is open, you can make changes to it. In your AUTOEXEC.BAT, you'll see these file markers. Place the changes you add to the file between them.

:DRDOSBEG   Marks the beginning of commands for DR DOS to interpret. Comments should be placed before this marker in the file.

:DRDOSEND   Marks the end of commands for DR DOS.

```
 c:\autoexec.bat  chr=1 col=1                                    ins  ^J=help
@ECHO OFF
REM The DRDOSBEG and DRDOSEND labels tell the SETUP program which
REM statements it should process. Put any additional statements for
REM DR DOS between these two labels. Any other statements e.g. for
REM other operating systems should be placed outside the labels.
:DRDOSBEG
PATH C:\;C:\DRDOS
VERIFY OFF
SHARE /L:20
PROMPT $P$G
MEMMAX +U >NUL
:DRDOSEND
```

Figure 13.2 The AUTOEXEC.BAT is ready to edit.

Place your cursor on the line below :DRDOSBEG before adding commands to your AUTOEXEC.BAT file. You will not see these markers in your CONFIG.SYS file.

There are many ways to move around the screen, here are the most commonly used methods:

To Move:	Press:
Up, down, left, or right	Arrow keys
To the beginning of a line	Ctrl+Q, then S
To the end of a line	Ctrl+Q, then D
Down one screen	Page Down
Up one screen	Page Up

When you start the DR DOS editor, you are in *insert mode.* That means that when you position your cursor and start to type, the text you type is inserted at that point, and all existing text is pushed to the right. If you want to type over existing characters, press the Insert key. You are now in *overtype mode.*

If you want to delete some characters, position your cursor on the first character and use the Delete key to delete one character at a time.

Saving Your File

After making changes to your file, you must save it before exiting the editor. With DR DOS, you have four options:

- *To save your file and exit EDITOR* Press Ctrl+K and then X.

- *To save your file and continue working* Press Ctrl+K and then S.

- *To save your file and begin editing another file* Press Ctrl+K and then D.

- *To abandon your changes and exit EDITOR* Press Ctrl+K and then Q. At the EDITOR title screen, press Esc.

In this lesson, you learned how to use the DR DOS editor. In the next lesson, you will learn how to use some of the DR DOS memory management commands.

Lesson 14

Managing Memory with DR DOS

In this lesson, you will learn how to use each of the DR DOS memory management commands.

Using the DR DOS Memory Management Commands

In earlier chapters, you've learned about the PC configuration files and how to edit them. You've learned about memory and how DR DOS can help you manage it. Now you're ready to roll up your sleeves and learn exactly how to take advantage of your new knowledge.

DR DOS's collection of memory management commands is called MemoryMAX, and it functions in a fashion similar to DOS 5 and DOS 6. DR DOS provides a simple setup program that you can use whenever you make changes to any of your configuration files. But to truly understand what is happening, you should read this lesson.

Know Your Options Some commands have many variations. In this lesson and the next, you will learn only the options for each command that are commonly used. Consult your DR DOS manual if you're interested in the advanced options.

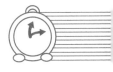

Reading Syntax To understand how to read the syntax that is given here for each command, review "Understanding the Syntax for Commands" in Lesson 11.

Using HIDOS.SYS

The device driver *HIDOS.SYS* is used in the CONFIG.SYS of 80286 machines to provide access to the high memory area. If you have a PC with a 386 or higher CPU, skip this section.

With the use of the HIDOS.SYS device driver, a portion of DR DOS, the *kernel*, is loaded into either upper or high memory.

Kernel The core of the disk operating system, which handles disk access and file management.

The command that loads the HIDOS.SYS driver *should be first* within the CONFIG.SYS. However, if your system loads a device driver that provides access to your hard drive, that command should be placed first, *just before* the HIDOS.SYS command. Also, if you are using any memory management software, make sure you load HIDOS.SYS *before* any memory management command.

HIDOS.SYS Syntax

The syntax for loading the HIDOS.SYS driver is:

```
DEVICE=[drive:\directory\]HIDOS.SYS
[/BDOS=AUTO¦FFFF¦nnnn¦NONE]
[/ROM=AUTO¦beg-end¦NONE]
```

The options (which appear in brackets) for loading HIDOS.SYS are:

drive:\directory   The drive and directory where the HIDOS.SYS file can be found, for example, C:\DRDOS\HIDOS.SYS.

This One's for You   The following HIDOS.SYS options are only available if your PC has specific RAM chip sets, upper memory blocks which follow the EMS 4.0 standard, or permanent unused areas of RAM (typically used to create shadow RAM).

/BDOS=AUTO¦FFFF¦*nnnn*¦NONE   Instructs HIDOS.SYS to load portions of the DR DOS operating system into upper or high memory. You can choose from several options:

AUTO   This is the default. Upper memory is scanned for a contiguous area big enough to hold the operating system kernel. If there is no area that is suitable, the FFFF address in high memory is used instead.

FFFF   Moves the DR DOS kernel to high memory address FFFF.

nnnn   Moves the DR DOS kernel to the specified address in upper memory (if there is enough room).

NONE   The DR DOS kernel is not moved.

/ROM=AUTO¦*beg-end*¦NONE   Causes the ROM BIOS routines to be copied to RAM, providing faster access. You can select from several options:

AUTO   Copies ROM to RAM.

beg-end Copies only the ROM found in the specified address to RAM.

NONE This is the default; it does not copy ROM into RAM.

HIDOS.SYS has several advanced options that can be used to specify:

- The high memory address range which is scanned to see if it is available for use by HIDOS.SYS.

- A high memory address range to be excluded from the scan.

- The release of high memory that is normally reserved for the Video Display Adapter.

- That certain addresses in upper memory not be tested, but be used anyway.

- That the extended BIOS data area be left at the top of conventional memory, and not be relocated by HIDOS.SYS to the bottom of conventional memory.

- Which chip set your PC uses.

HIDOS.SYS Examples

The simplest way to load HIDOS is with the command:

```
DEVICE=C:\DRDOS\HIDOS.SYS /BDOS=AUTO
```

To load HIDOS and have it move the DR DOS kernel to high memory, use this command:

```
DEVICE=C:\DRDOS\HIDOS.SYS /BDOS=FFFF
```

To load HIDOS, have it move the DR DOS kernel into upper memory, and copy ROM BIOS into RAM, use this command:

```
DEVICE=C:\DRDOS\HIDOS.SYS /BDOS=AUTO /ROM=AUTO
```

Using EMM386.SYS

The EMM386.SYS driver is used in the CONFIG.SYS of machines that have at least an 80386 CPU. The EMM386 device driver:

- Fills UMBs (upper memory blocks) with expanded memory so that device drivers and TSRs can be loaded there.

- Provides access to extended memory for programs that use it.

- Simulates expanded memory with extended memory.

- Moves the DR DOS kernel to high or upper memory.

- Creates shadow RAM.

Shadow RAM   RAM in upper memory which is filled with a copy of the ROM BIOS routines, enabling faster access. Some PCs do not have the capability to create shadow RAM.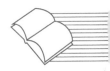

EMM386 is loaded through the CONFIG.SYS file, and it *should be first* within the CONFIG.SYS. However, if your system loads a device driver that provides access to your hard drive, that command should be placed first, *just before* the EMM386.SYS command. Also, if you are using

91

any memory management software, make sure you load EMM386.SYS *before* any memory management command.

EMM386.SYS Syntax

The syntax for loading the EMM386.SYS driver is:

```
DEVICE=[drive:\directory\]EMM386.SYS
[/FRAME=AUTO¦NONE¦nnnn]
[/KB=0¦AUTO\nnnn] [/BDOS=AUTO¦FFFF¦nnnn¦NONE]
```

The options (which appear in brackets) for loading EMM386.SYS are:

drive:\directory   The drive and directory where the EMM386.SYS file can be found, for example, C:\DRDOS\EMM386.SYS.

/FRAME=AUTO¦NONE¦*nnnn*   Instructs EMM386.SYS to create a 64K page frame in upper memory. Choose from these options:

AUTO   The default; causes EMM386.SYS to create a 64K page frame in upper memory.

NONE   Access to extended memory is allowed, but the page frame (for expanded memory) is not created.

nnnn   Creates the 64K page frame at the specified address.

/KB=0¦AUTO*nnnn*   Determines the amount of extended memory used in creating expanded memory. Choose from these options:

0 or AUTO   Uses all of extended memory.

nnnn   Uses the specified amount (in K) of extended memory.

/BDOS=AUTO¦FFFF¦*nnnn*¦NONE   Instructs EMM386.SYS to load portions of the DR DOS operating system into upper or high memory. You can choose from several options:

AUTO   This is the default. Upper memory is scanned for a contiguous area big enough to hold the operating system kernel. If there is no area that is suitable, the FFFF address in high memory is used instead.

FFFF   Moves the DR DOS kernel to high memory address FFFF.

nnnn   Moves the DR DOS kernel to the specified address in upper memory (if there is enough room).

NONE   The DR DOS kernel is not moved.

EMM386.SYS has several advanced options that can be used to specify:

- The high memory address range to be scanned to see if it is available for use by EMM386.SYS for loading DOS, device drivers, and TSRs.

- A high memory address range to be excluded from the scan.

- The release of high memory that is normally reserved for the Video Display Adapter.

- That certain addresses in upper memory not be tested, but be used anyway.

- That the extended BIOS data area be left at the top of conventional memory, and not be relocated by HIDOS.SYS to the bottom of conventional memory.

- That the ROM BIOS routines be copied to RAM, providing faster access.

- That with Compaq 386 and 486 machines, an additional 256K extended memory be made available.

- That EMM386.SYS leave itself in conventional memory, freeing upper memory for use by the page frame and other devices, such as a network adapter card.

- That EMM386.SYS work with Windows 3.0 in standard mode.

EMM386.SYS Examples

To load the DR DOS kernel and its data structures into upper memory in order to create upper memory blocks but no expanded memory, use:

```
DEVICE=C:\DRDOS\EMM386.SYS /FRAME=NONE
/BDOS=AUTO DOS=ON
```

Once upper memory blocks are created, you can load device drivers and TSRs into them. Extended memory, in this example, is used by programs that are designed to use it, such as Windows.

To create upper memory blocks and 4MB of expanded memory, while moving DOS and its data structures into upper memory, use:

```
DEVICE=C:\DRDOS\EMM386.SYS /FRAME=AUTO /KB=4096
/BDOS=AUTO HIDOS=ON
```

To create upper memory blocks and 2MB of expanded memory, move DOS and its data structures into upper memory, and to relocate the page frame to the E000h address, use:

```
DEVICE=C:\DRDOS\EMM386.SYS /FRAME=E000 /KB=2048
/BDOS=AUTO HIDOS=ON
```

Freeing More Upper Memory To make the most upper memory available for device drivers and TSRs, use the /BDOS=FFFF option to force the DR DOS kernel to be placed in high memory instead of upper memory.

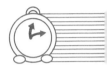

Using EMMXMA.SYS

Like EMM386.SYS and HIDOS.SYS, the EMMXMA. SYS driver simulates expanded memory. It is used with IBM PS/2 computers, in the CONFIG.SYS. If you don't have a PS/2 PC, you can skip this section.

EMMXMA.SYS Syntax

The syntax for loading the EMM386.SYS driver is:

```
DEVICE=[drive:\directory\]EMMXMA.SYS
[/FRAME=nnnn] [/KB=nnnn]
```

The options (which appear in brackets) for loading EMMXMA.SYS are:

drive:\directory The drive and directory where the EMM386.SYS file can be found, for example, C:\DRDOS\EMMXMA.SYS.

/FRAME=*nnnn*   Instructs EMMXMA.SYS to create a 64KB page frame at the specified address in upper memory. If you do not specify this option, the address C000h is used.

/KB=*nnnn*   Determines the amount of extended memory (in K) used to create expanded memory. If you do not specify this option, all of extended memory is used.

Third Party Problems?   You cannot use the EMMXMA.SYS driver with third party memory managers.

EMMXMA.SYS Examples

To create 4MB of expanded memory, use:

```
C:\DRDOS\EMMXMA.SYS  /KB=4096
```

In this lesson, you learned three basic DR DOS memory management commands. In the next lesson, you will learn how to load DOS, device drivers, and TSRs high, out of conventional memory into upper and high memory.

Lesson 15

Maximizing Conventional Memory with DR DOS

In this lesson, you will learn how to use DR DOS to load the DOS data structures, device drivers, and TSRs into upper memory.

Using the HIDOS Command

The HIDOS command is used somewhere in the CONFIG.SYS *after* the HIDOS.SYS or EMM386.SYS command, to load the DOS data structures (such as BUFFERS) into upper memory.

Deja Vu? DR DOS has made things a bit confusing by including a HIDOS.SYS device driver (to be used with 286 CPUs exclusively) and a HIDOS configuration command in its vocabulary, but I will try to keep things clear. Regardless of whether you use the HIDOS.SYS or the EMM386.SYS device driver, you will need the HIDOS command to load the DOS data structures into upper memory.

97

HIDOS Syntax

The syntax for using the HIDOS command is:

```
HIDOS=ON|OFF
```

The options for loading HIDOS are:

ON or OFF Controls whether the DOS data structures load into upper memory. If you specify ON, DOS data structures load into upper memory. If you specify OFF, DOS loads into conventional memory. The default is OFF.

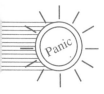

Third Party Conflicts The HIDOS command cannot be used with third-party memory managers such as QEMM-386 or QRAM. You'll learn more about these third-party products in Lesson 22.

HIDOS Examples

To load DOS and its data structures into the upper memory area, you need two commands. If you have a 286 PC, use these commands:

```
DEVICE=C:\DRDOS\HIDOS.SYS /BDOS=AUTO
HIDOS=ON
```

If you have a 386 PC or above, use these commands:

```
DEVICE=C:\DRDOS\EMM386.SYS /BDOS=AUTO
HIDOS=ON
```

Using the HIDEVICE Command

Use the HIDEVICE command in your CONFIG.SYS to load device drivers into upper memory. Before using the HIDEVICE command, you must create upper memory blocks by loading either HIDOS.SYS (for 286 computers) or EMM386.SYS (for 386 and 486 computers). If a device driver is too big to fit into upper memory, it loads into conventional memory automatically.

Line Up! Use the MEM command, described in Lesson 4, to verify which of your device drivers is the largest, and load them according to size (from largest to smallest).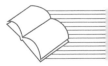

HIDEVICE estimates the size of a device driver and loads it into an appropriate open space in upper memory. However, some device drivers request additional memory after they have been loaded, and they can cause your system to lock up. To estimate the actual amount a device driver needs, load it into conventional memory (using the DEVICE command), reboot, and then use the MEM command to view the driver's size. You can then specify the amount of memory to be assigned to a particular device driver through the SIZE option, discussed in the next section.

HIDEVICE Syntax

The syntax for using the HIDEVICE command is:

```
HIDEVICE=[SIZE=size][drive:\directory\]driverfilename
```

The options (which appear in brackets) for using HIDEVICE are:

99

SIZE=*size* Use *size* (in hexadecimal) to specify the minimum amount of upper memory required to load this device. A device will not be loaded if the minimum amount specified is not available. If *size* is not specified, DR DOS estimates the amount of upper memory to allocate.

drive:\directory The drive and directory where the device driver is found, for example, C:\DRDOS\ANSI.SYS.

HIDEVICE Examples

To simulate expanded memory, the following command moves the DR DOS kernel into high memory, moves DR DOS data structures into upper memory, and loads the device driver, ANSI.SYS, into upper memory for a 386 PC or above:

```
DEVICE=C:\DRDOS\EMM386.SYS /FRAME=AUTO  BDOS=FFFF
HIDOS=ON
HIDEVICE=C:\DRDOS\ANSI.SYS
```

To simulate expanded memory, this command moves the DR DOS kernel into high memory, moves DR DOS data structures into upper memory, and loads the device driver, ANSI.SYS, into upper memory for a 286 PC:

```
DEVICE=C:\DRDOS\HIDOS.SYS /BDOS=FFFF
HIDOS=ON
HIDEVICE=C:\DRDOS\ANSI.SYS
```

Using the HIINSTALL Command

Use the HIINSTALL command in your CONFIG.SYS to load TSRs (and certain DR DOS commands) into upper memory. Most TSRs are loaded through commands in the AUTOEXEC.BAT—those TSRs require the use of the HILOAD command covered in the next section. Before using the HIINSTALL command, you must create upper memory blocks by loading either the HIDOS.SYS or EMM386.SYS drivers.

HIINSTALL Syntax

The syntax for using the HIINSTALL command is:

```
HIINSTALL=[drive:\directory\]driverfilename
[options]
```

The options (which appear in brackets) for using HIINSTALL are:

drive:\directory The drive and directory where the TSR or DR DOS command are found, for example, C:\DRDOS\CURSOR.EXE.

HIINSTALL Examples

To load CURSOR.EXE into upper memory, include these commands in your CONFIG.SYS if you have a 386 PC or above:

```
DEVICE=C:\DRDOS\EMM386.SYS /FRAME=AUTO /BDOS=FFFF
```

```
HIDOS=ON
HIINSTALL=C:\DRDOS\CURSOR.EXE
```

If you own a 286 PC, use these commands:

```
DEVICE=C:\DRDOS\HIDOS.SYS /BDOS=FFFF
HIDOS=ON
HIINSTALL=C:\DRDOS\CURSOR.EXE
```

Using the HILOAD Command

Use the HILOAD command to load TSRs (and certain DR DOS commands) into upper memory. Before using the HILOAD command, you must create upper memory blocks by loading either the HIDOS.SYS or EMM386.SYS drivers.

Unlike the HIINSTALL command, which is used in the CONFIG.SYS file, the HILOAD command is used in the AUTOEXEC.BAT file. TSRs and other programs loaded with the HILOAD command load after both the commands in CONFIG.SYS and COMMAND.COM.

HILOAD Syntax

The syntax for using the HILOAD command is:

```
HILOAD=[drive:\directory\]driverfilename
```

The options (which appear in brackets) for using HILOAD are:

drive:\directory   The drive and directory where the TSR or DR DOS command is found, for example, C:\DRDOS\CURSOR.EXE.

HILOAD Examples

To load CURSOR.EXE into upper memory after the commands in CONFIG.SYS have been processed and COMMAND.COM has been loaded, include these commands in your CONFIG.SYS if you have a 386 PC or above:

```
DEVICE=C:\DRDOS\EMM386.SYS /FRAME=AUTO BDOS=FFFF
HIDOS=ON
```

Include the following commands in your CONFIG.SYS if you have a 286 PC:

```
DEVICE=C:\DRDOS\EMM386.SYS /BDOS=FFFF
HIDOS=ON
```

Once you have the proper commands in your CONFIG.SYS, include this command in your AUTOEXEC.BAT:

```
HILOAD=C:\DRDOS\CURSOR.EXE
```

In this lesson, you learned how to use DR DOS to load the DOS data structures, device drivers, and TSRs into upper memory. In the next lesson, you will learn how to maximize your system's memory.

Lesson 16
RAM-Saving Strategies

In this lesson, you will learn how to maximize RAM by removing programs you don't need, and moving as much as you can out of conventional memory and into upper and high memory.

In the last few lessons, you've learned how to use the MS-DOS or DR DOS editor. You've also learned the proper syntax for the DOS memory management commands. There are some other DOS commands that are assigned RAM by default, which you can remove to maximize your system's memory use. Let's learn about some of them.

Another Look at Your CONFIG.SYS

When you try maximizing your PC's use of memory, there are many areas in which you can look. One of these areas is the CONFIG.SYS file.

Evaluating the Importance of Device Drivers

There are many device drivers that you might find in your
CONFIG.SYS. Some are important, some are not. Print out
a copy of your CONFIG.SYS using the instructions in
Lesson 6 and compare it to this list of common device
drivers:

ANSI.SYS   This device driver is by far the most
common, yet you may not need it. The purpose of this
device driver is to enhance your keyboard and monitor
usage. If you have special batch files or programs that
use the extended capabilities of your keyboard or monitor, you will need to keep this device driver in your
CONFIG.SYS. How can you tell if you need ANSI.SYS?
Check your program manuals or simply delete the line
from your CONFIG.SYS, reboot, and run a test on all
your programs. If you don't run into a problem, you
didn't need ANSI.SYS.

MOUSE.SYS   This device driver (and similar ones)
are used to provide access to a mouse. If you no longer
use a mouse with your system, you can delete this
device driver.

NAV_.SYS   This device driver comes with Norton
Anti-Virus. I use it to check my system around the clock
for the presence of viruses. If you have a virus detection
program, you may have a device driver like this or
another, such as VSAFE.SYS, which is part of the
Central Point Anti-Virus program. I would not delete it.

STACKER.SYS   This device driver (and others like
it) is used to compress (make smaller) the files on your
hard disk, until they are needed by a program. By using
disk compression programs, you can keep more files on

your hard disk in a smaller amount of space. If you use one of these device drivers, do not remove it. Like the device driver above, it provides access to the files on your hard disk.

Removing Device Drivers from Conventional Memory

If your system has extended memory and UMBs have been provided through the use of HIMEM.SYS and the DOS command, be sure to make the following changes:

```
DEVICEHIGH=C:\BIN\NAV\NAV_.SYS
DEVICEHIGH=C:\DOS\ANSI.SYS
DEVICEHIGH=C:\WINDOWS\MOUSE.SYS
```

If you are using DR DOS, you should make these changes instead:

```
HIDEVICE=C:\BIN\NAV\NAV_.SYS
HIDEVICE=C:\DOS\ANSI.SYS
HIDEVICE=C:\WINDOWS\MOUSE.SYS
```

These changes move the device drivers into upper memory.

Scared of "HIGH"ts Not all device drivers can be loaded into UMB's. Change DEVICE= to DEVICEHIGH= one statement at a time, then reboot and use MEM /C to see if the device driver loaded correctly. If it did, go on to the next device driver in your CONFIG.SYS. Make sure you have your boot diskette handy should any of these drivers lock up your system.

Here is a list of some of the MS-DOS 5, MS-DOS 6, and DR DOS device drivers that can be loaded into UMBs:

MS-DOS 5 and 6	*DR DOS*
DISPLAY.SYS	ANSI.SYS
DRIVER.SYS	DISPLAY.SYS
EGA.SYS	PRINTER.SYS
ANSI.SYS	VDISK.SYS
PRINTER.SYS	
RAMDRIVE.SYS	
SETVER.EXE	
SMARTDRV.SYS	

Miscellaneous CONFIG.SYS Commands That Use RAM

In Lesson 6, you learned that some DOS commands in your CONFIG.SYS use RAM. These include:

- FILES
- FCBS
- BUFFERS
- STACKS
- SHELL

Minimizing the amount of RAM used by these commands provides effective memory management:

FILES   Uses from 40–60 bytes of conventional memory per file; 20 is usually a good number. With some multitasking environments, such as Windows and GeoWorks, use 30. Some third-party memory managers can move FILES into upper memory. The default is 8.

FCBS   Uses from 40–60 bytes of conventional memory per file control block; may be set to 1 if you are not on a network. The default is 4.

BUFFERS   Uses about 512 bytes of conventional memory per buffer; 10–20 is usually a good number. If you use a disk caching program such as SMARTDRV, set the number of buffers to 3. Default varies by system. The DOS=HIGH or HIDOS=ON commands move the DOS data structures (buffers) into high memory.

STACKS   The default of 9,126 on most systems uses about 1K of conventional memory. You can usually set STACKS to zero.

SHELL   Enlarges the environment area when an error message indicates that it is too small. One way to reduce environment area usage is to shorten your PATH statement, as discussed in the next section on AUTOEXEC.BAT.

Suppose your CONFIG.SYS contains these lines:

```
STACKS=9,256
FILES=40
BUFFERS=40
```

We may want to make the following changes. (Check with your software documentation before making changes to the number of FILES, and test your system to determine the optimum number of BUFFERS.)

```
STACKS=0,0
FILES=20
BUFFERS=30
```

Another Look at Your AUTOEXEC.BAT

There are many commands in your AUTOEXEC.BAT which can use RAM. Use the instructions in Lesson 6 to print a copy of your AUTOEXEC.BAT, and compare it to this sample, which contains many typical commands:

```
C:\WINDOWS\SMARTDRV.EXE
@ECHO OFF
CLS
PATH=C:\WINDOWS;C:\DOS;C:\NC;C:\WORD;C:\FASTBAC;
C:\NORTON;C:\NAV;C:\ZIP;C:\FAR
PROMPT $P$G
SET TEMP=C:\WINDOWS\TEMP
SET TEMP=C:\WINDOWS\TEMP
SET FASTBACK=C:\FASTBACK
SET PCPLUS=C:\PCPLUS
C:\SIDEKICK\SK2
```

The first command in our AUTOEXEC.BAT file creates a RAM disk. The benefits of creating a RAM disk will be discussed in Lesson 19. Let's look at some of the other lines in the next few sections.

Following Your Own PATH

The PATH statement included in your AUTOEXEC.BAT loads into the environment area in RAM. If your environment area gets too full (the default size will hold 128 characters), you might decide to enlarge it with the SHELL command. Before you consider enlarging the environment area, make sure that you need all of the directories in your PATH statement.

The PATH statement provides DOS with a list of directories to search for command files not located in the current directory. The PATH statement provides convenience, but at a cost. If you do not actually use all of the programs listed in the PATH statement, you should delete them. You can also create batch files placed in a single directory (such as \BATCH), which start each program for you. Then your path statement can be shortened to:

```
PATH=C:\WINDOWS;C:\DOS;C:\BATCH
```

You should always include a PATH to \DOS (and \WINDOWS, if you use that program).

Miscellaneous AUTOEXEC.BAT Commands That Use RAM

Table 16.1 lists some of the commands in your AUTOEXEC.BAT which use RAM, and what to do about them.

Table 16.1 Commands in your AUTOEXEC.BAT that use RAM.

Command	Problem	What to do
PATH	Loads into the environment area	Place these commands after commands which call TSRs, to reduce the size of the environment that TSRs are given.
PROMPT	Same as PATH	
SET	Same as PATH	
TSRs	They are given a copy of the environment file when they load.	Load TSRs first in your AUTOEXEC.BAT, and use LOADHIGH or HILOAD.

Using the table as a guide, we could make the following changes to the sample AUTOEXEC.BAT. (If you use DR DOS, substitute HILOAD for the LOADHIGH command.)

```
C:\WINDOWS\SMARTDRV.EXE
@ECHO OFF
CLS
LOADHIGH C:\SIDEKICK\SK2
PATH=C:\WINDOWS;C:\DOS;C:\BATCH
PROMPT $P$G
SET TEMP=C:\WINDOWS\TEMP
SET TMP=C:\WINDOWS\TEMP
SET FASTBACK=C:\FASTBACK
SET PCPLUS=C:\PCPLUS
```

In this lesson, you learned several techniques for maximizing your system's memory use. In the next lesson, you will learn how to maximize your system's memory when you use Windows.

Powerful Memory Management with Windows

In this lesson, you will learn how to maximize Windows management of memory.

How Windows Handles Memory

Windows 3.1 and Windows for Workgroups runs in two modes—*standard* (for 286 PCs) and *enhanced* (for 386 PCs and above). Windows determines the best operating mode for your PC, and automatically starts in that mode. In each mode, Windows handles memory in a slightly different fashion.

Windows and Standard Mode

When running in standard mode, Windows only uses conventional memory and extended memory. In standard mode, Windows can't grab UMBs from EMM386, so upper memory is wasted except for whatever use DOS can make of it. Windows combines conventional and extended memory into one big "memory pool" which is divided among the programs that run under Windows.

In standard mode, existing expanded memory is ignored unless a DOS application requests it. Windows then acts as an intermediary between DOS and the application, passing the requests for expanded memory to DOS.

When the pool of available memory runs low, Windows starts swapping unused files out to the hard drive, then swapping them back again when they're requested. The swap file that Windows creates on the hard drive is called *virtual memory*. Virtual memory is not real memory (it's the hard disk), but it gets its name because, to programs at least, it appears to be memory. Files that programs think are in memory are really being kept on the hard disk until needed.

Virtual Memory   Memory that does not exist, but is simulated by using hard disk space.

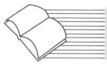

If a DOS application is run under Windows standard mode, all activity is suspended until that DOS application is exited.

Windows and Enhanced Mode

When running in enhanced mode, Windows again uses conventional and extended memory. If an application requests expanded memory, it is created out of extended memory by Windows and EMM386. Any existing expanded memory is ignored by Windows.

In standard mode, Windows can't grab upper memory blocks (UMBs) from EMM386, so they go unused. In enhanced mode, because of the increased capabilities of the CPU, UMBs can be used by Windows, and they are incorporated into the memory pool.

Pool's Open In standard mode, you can provide unused UMBs to Windows by using the /EXCLUDE parameter with EMM386.EXE in your CONFIG.SYS file to exclude areas of upper memory from EMM386's domain. To determine which areas of upper memory are unused, use the MEM command (see Lesson 4).

In standard mode, DOS applications temporarily suspend all other functions until they are exited. In enhanced mode, a *virtual machine* is created for each DOS application run.

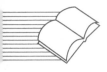

Virtual Machine A virtual machine is a complete DOS environment constructed out of a space in extended memory. Windows takes advantage of the 386/486 CPU's capability to slice extended memory into 640K chunks to create several "computers" or virtual machines.

When each virtual machine is created (one for each active DOS application and one for Windows), a copy of the DOS environment is made. If you load a TSR when the PC is booted, that TSR will be copied to each virtual machine and made available. This is fine if you intend to use that TSR with several DOS applications. If you use the TSR for Windows applications only, do not load the TSR through the AUTOEXEC.BAT or CONFIG.SYS, because you will waste memory.

Like TSRs, device drivers also get copied to each virtual machine, so it is important to load them into UMBs to keep them from wasting memory.

How to Streamline Your Configuration Files for Windows

There are several things you can do to streamline your configuration files for Windows:

- Use all of extended memory as extended, not expanded, memory. Windows cannot make use of any expanded memory unless it is running in standard mode. (Even then, expanded memory will be used only for DOS applications that specifically request it.) For MS-DOS, use the following:

```
DEVICE=C:\DOS\EMM386.EXE NOEMS
```

  or for DR DOS:

```
DEVICE=C:\DRDOS\EMM386.SYS /FRAME=NONE
/BDOS=FFFF
```

- Set FILES to about 30. Experiment for best results.

- Set BUFFERS to about 30 if you are not using SMARTDRV (described in Lesson 18), or anywhere from 1–15 if you are. Experiment for the best results.

- If you must load a device driver, put it onto a UMB. For MS-DOS use:

```
C:\DOS\HIMEM.SYS
DOS=HIGH,UMB
DEVICE=C:\DOS\EMM386.EXE NOEMS
DEVICEHIGH=C:\DOS\ANSI.SYS
```

115

or for DR DOS:

```
DEVICE=C:\DRDOS\EMM386.SYS /FRAME=NONE /BDOS=FFFF
HIDOS=ON
HIDEVICE=C:\DRDOS\ANSI.SYS
```

- With the following line, set STACKS to zero, because Windows does not need the STACKS statement.

```
STACKS=0,0
```

- In the AUTOEXEC.BAT, load TSRs into UMBs (or consider loading them through the WINSTART.BAT if the TSRs are to be used with Windows programs only). For MS-DOS:

```
LOADHIGH=C:\DOS\DOSKEY
```

or for DR DOS:

```
HILOAD=C:\DRDOS\CURSOR.EXE
```

DR DOS and Windows

Special issues arise when using Windows with DR DOS. During setup, choose the option that lets you review changes being made to your AUTOEXEC.BAT and CONFIG.SYS. Look for these items:

- In your AUTOEXEC.BAT, remove the reference to SMARTDRV. This should be replaced with the Super PC-Kwik disk caching utility that comes with DR DOS. You will learn about disk caching in Lesson 18.

- In your CONFIG.SYS, replace the reference to HIMEM.SYS with either HIDOS.SYS or EMM386.SYS.

In this lesson, you learned how to maximize your memory usage when using Windows. In the next lesson, you will learn how to create a disk cache.

Lesson 18

Caching In on a Good Thing

In this lesson, you will learn about disk caches and how you can use them effectively.

What Is a Disk Cache?

A *disk cache* is a buffer in memory that stores copies of information read from the hard disk (see Figure 18.1). If the same information is requested later, it is read from RAM (a very fast process), rather than the hard disk (a very slow process). When the cache gets full, the least requested information is overwritten, ensuring that only the most needed information is kept in the cache.

Disk Cache   An area of RAM which stores the most often used disk data for faster access.

Some popular disk cache programs include SMARTDRV (which comes with DOS 5, DOS 6, and Windows), Super PC-Kwik (which comes with DR DOS), Hyperdisk, Norton Cache, Memory Commander's cache, and Quadtel's cache.

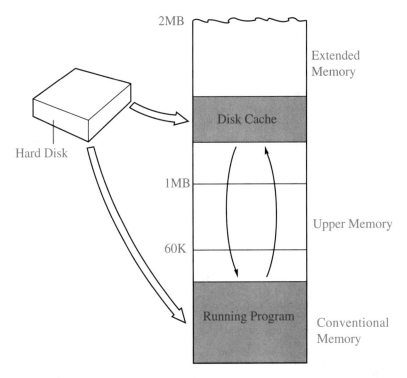

Figure 18.1 A disk cache stores data read from the hard disk for later use by the running program.

Some disk caches (such as SMARTDRV) do not cache floppy disk operations, so you may still want a BUFFERS statement in your CONFIG.SYS. Try setting BUFFERS to 10, and if floppy disk operations appear to be significantly slower, increase this number by 10 until you have an optimal environment. Other disk caches (such as Super PC-Kwik) do provide floppy disk buffering. So set BUFFERS to 5 when working with these products.

119

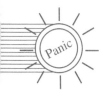

Do Not Optimize When Using a Cache You should not run a disk optimization utility when using a cache. (A disk optimization utility rearranges files on your hard drive so that disk access times improves.)

Improving the Performance of Your Hard Disk with SMARTDRV

MS-DOS 5 and 6 both come with the disk caching program SMARTDRV. The cache is created using extended memory, unless the /A parameter is used, and then expanded memory is utilized. SMARTDRV provides two services. It acts as a disk cache when loaded from the AUTOEXEC.BAT file, and it provides double-buffering services for drives that need it, if loaded from the CONFIG.SYS file.

If your hard drive is SCSI, ESDI, or another drive identified as needing SMARTDRV's double-buffering services, you should load SMARTDRV into both your CONFIG.SYS and AUTOEXEC.BAT files to enable disk caching *and* double-buffering. If you're not sure, see your DOS documentation.

Setting Up Double-Buffering

If your hard drive requires double-buffering, and you've installed Windows 3.1 or DOS 6, chances are good that an installation program has already set up double-buffering for you. Look for this line in your CONFIG.SYS; if it's not there, add it.

```
DEVICEHIGH=C:\DOS\SMARTDRV.EXE /double_buffer
```

Don't confuse this method with the enabling of a disk cache, which is done by loading SMARTDRV from the AUTOEXEC.BAT file.

Creating a Disk Cache with SMARTDRV

You use SMARTDRV to make a disk cache when loaded from your AUTOEXEC.BAT file. Don't confuse this use of SMARTDRV with one we just learned about in the previous section. If you run SMARTDRV from your CONFIG.SYS file, you can only use it to double-buffer a hard drive that needs this special service. If you run SMARTDRV from your AUTOEXEC.BAT file, it is useful for creating a disk cache.

Use this command to use SMARTDRV to create a disk cache:

```
[drive:\directory\]SMARTDRV.EXE
[DOScache][WINcache]
```

Listed here are the options that are commonly used. Consult your Windows manual if you're interested in the advanced options.

drive:\directory The drive and directory where the SMARTDRV.EXE file is found, for example, C:\WINDOWS\SMARTDRV.EXE.

DOScache This number specifies the size (in K) of extended memory the cache should occupy prior to Windows starting.

WINcache This number specifies the minimum size (in K) of extended memory that the cache can occupy once Windows has started. Windows will try to reduce the

121

cache size if it needs the memory occupied by the cache. This entry sets a minimum that Windows can't supercede. It's a sort of "safety net."

Just My Size If you don't specify the size of the *DOScache*, SMARTDRV.EXE will estimate the amount needed, based on the amount of extended memory available.

For example, if you had 2–4MB of extended memory, and wanted to create a disk cache with a 2MB DOS size, and minimum size of 1MB under Windows, place this command in your AUTOEXEC.BAT:

```
C:\WINDOWS\SMARTDRV.EXE 2048 1024
```

Creating a Disk Cache with Super PC-Kwik

You can create a disk cache in DR DOS in two steps. You must first add a DEVICE (or HIDEVICE) command to the CONFIG.SYS:

```
DEVICE=[drive:\directory\]PCKWIK.SYS
```

The options (which appear in brackets) for loading PCKWIK.SYS include many variations. Listed here are the options that are commonly used. Consult your DR DOS manual if you're interested in the advanced options.

Easy Setup You can install Super PC-Kwik using the DR DOS setup program, and it automatically makes changes to your AUTOEXEC.BAT and your CONFIG.SYS. There are many advanced options for using Super PC-Kwik that are available through the setup program.

122

drive:\directory The drive and directory where the PCKWIK.SYS file can be found, for example, C:\DRDOS\PCKWIK.SYS.

When you have created the disk cache, in your AUTOEXEC.BAT file include the command:

```
[drive:\directory\]SUPERPCK [/&U+¦-] [/A+] [/EM+]
[/L:mmmm¦-]
```

The options (which appear in brackets) for loading SUPERPCK are:

drive:\directory The drive and directory where the SUPERPCK.EXE file is found, for example, C:\DRDOS\SUPERPCK.EXE.

/&U+|- Determines whether SUPERPCK is placed in upper memory. Default is /&U+ or yes.

/A+ Uses expanded memory for the cache.

/EM+ Uses extended memory for the cache. If you use Windows, use this option.

/L:*mmmm*¦- Sets the amount of memory (in K) SUPERPCK lends to other programs. If you use Windows, set this number to the maximum amount, or at least 2,048. To prevent any memory from being lent, use /L-.

In this lesson, you learned what a disk cache is and how to create one. In the next lesson, you will learn how to create a RAM disk.

Lesson 19

Speeding Up Your Hard Disk with RAM

In this lesson, you will learn what a RAM disk is and how to create one.

What Is a RAM Disk?

A *RAM disk* is a disk drive created in memory. A RAM disk looks and acts like any other disk drive (such as C:), but the computer can quickly read and write information to it because it is made out of memory (see Figure 19.1). However, because a RAM disk is made of memory, its data is erased when the PC is turned off.

Treat a RAM disk like any other disk drive; you can copy files, delete files, make directories, and so on.

There are many popular RAM disk utilities, including RAMDRIVE, VDISK, Memory Commander RAM disk, and Quadtel RAM disk.

Once You Create Your RAM Disk   Be sure to include the statement SET TEMP=D:\ in your AUTOEXEC.BAT (assuming your RAM disk is drive D:). This tells your applications where to place their temporary files.

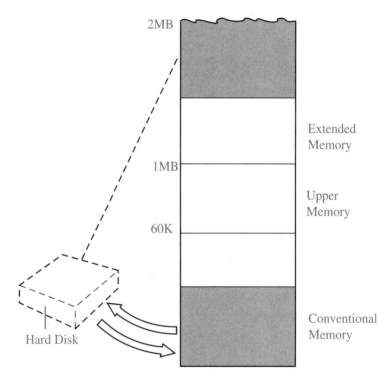

Figure 19.1   A RAM disk functions as a very fast, but temporary, hard disk.

Creating a RAM Disk with RAMDRIVE.SYS

RAMDRIVE.SYS comes with DOS 5, DOS 6 and Windows 3.1. Prior versions provided a utility called VDISK.SYS instead, which accomplished much the same thing.

RAMDRIVE can be used to create a RAM disk in either conventional, expanded, or extended memory. (Conventional is the default.) The syntax for loading the RAMDRIVE.SYS driver is:

125

```
DEVICE[HIGH]=[drive:\directory\]RAMDRIVE.SYS
[disksize]
[sectorsize] [direntries] [/E] [/A]
```

The options (which appear in brackets) for loading RAMDRIVE.SYS.EXE are:

drive:\directory The drive and directory where RAMDRIVE.SYS is found, for example, C:\DOS\RAMDRIVE.SYS.

disksize The size of the RAM disk in K. Allowable values are from 16 to 4,096; default is 64.

sectorsize The size of the sectors (in bytes) used for the RAM disk. Allowable values are 128, 256, and 512; default is 512. If you use this parameter, you must also specify *disksize*.

direntries Puts a limit on the number of files and directories that can be placed in the root directory of the RAM disk. Allowable values are from 2 to 1,024; default is 64. If you use this parameter, you must also specify *disksize* and *sectorsize*.

/E Tells RAMDRIVE to place the RAM disk in extended memory.

/A Tells RAMDRIVE to place the RAM disk in expanded memory.

For example, to install a 2MB RAM disk in extended memory, add this statement to your CONFIG.SYS:

```
DEVICEHIGH=C:\DOS\RAMDRIVE.SYS 2048 /E
```

Creating a RAM Disk with VDISK.SYS

VDISK.SYS comes with DR DOS and DOS versions prior to DOS 5. If you use MS-DOS 5 or 6, use RAMDRIVE.SYS to create your RAM disk. VDISK can be used to create a RAM disk in either conventional, expanded, or extended memory. (Conventional is the default.) The syntax for loading the VDISK.SYS driver is:

```
[HI]DEVICE=[drive:\directory\]VDISK.SYS
[disksize]
[sectorsize] [direntries] [/E[:sectors]]
[/X[:sectors]]
```

The options (which appear in brackets) for loading VDISK.SYS.EXE are:

drive:\directory   The drive and directory where VDISK.SYS is found, for example, C:\DRDOS\VDISK.SYS.

disksize   The size of the RAM disk in K. Allowable values range from 1 up to the size of your system's memory; default is 64.

sectorsize   The size of the sectors (in bytes) used for the RAM disk. Allowable values are 128, 256, and 512; default is 512. If you use this parameter, you must also specify *disksize*.

direntries   Puts a limit on the number of files and directories that can be placed in the root directory of the RAM disk. Allowable values are from 2 to 512; default is 64. If you use this parameter, you must also specify *disksize* and *sectorsize*.

127

/E:*sectors* Tells VDISK to place the RAM disk in extended memory. The optional *sectors* parameter determines the number of sectors transferred between conventional and extended memory at one time. Allowable values are from 1 to 8; the default is 8. Experiment with this number if you encounter trouble getting VDISK to work with extended memory.

/X Tells VDISK to place the RAM disk in expanded memory. The optional *sectors* parameter determines the number of sectors transferred between conventional and extended memory at one time. Allowable values are from 1 to 8; the default is 8. Experiment with this number if you encounter trouble getting VDISK to work with expanded memory. DR DOS does not provide the *sectors* option.

For example, if you are using MS-DOS version 4.0 or lower, and you want to create a RAM disk of 2MB in extended memory, include this statement in your CONFIG.SYS:

```
DEVICE=C:\DOS\VDISK.SYS 2048 /E
```

If you are using DR DOS and you want to create a RAM disk of 1MB in expanded memory, include this statement in your CONFIG.SYS:

```
HIDEVICE=C:\DRDOS\VDISK.SYS 1024 /X
```

In this lesson, you learned what a RAM disk is and how to create one. In the next lesson, you will learn memory management strategies to apply to your specific PC.

Lesson 20

Bottom-Line Strategies for Your System

In this lesson, you will learn some memory management strategies that you can apply specifically to your PC.

If You Own an 8088/8086 PC

If you own a PC with an 8088 or an 8086 CPU, your memory management options are severely limited. However, here are a few recommendations:

- Consider using an expanded memory board to add additional expanded memory to your system. Because these boards often come with extras, you can cheaply add serial/parallel ports and an internal clock to your system.

- If you purchase a memory board, be sure that it can "backfill" (bring your system's base memory up to 640K), if necessary.

- Consider purchasing a third-party memory management program, such as QRAM and 386MAX version 6.x (386MAX includes a program called MOVE'EM, which is designed for 8088/8086/80286 PCs, and used to be sold separately), to provide memory management support for expanded memory boards.

- Create a disk cache or a RAM disk with expanded memory to improve system speed.

- Consider whether to upgrade your system to a faster CPU or to purchase a whole new system. Prices vary, but in most cases, upgrading or buying a new system will prove a better investment than adding memory to your existing system.

If You Own a 286 PC

If you own a PC with a 286 CPU, there are not a lot of options for you as far as memory management is concerned. However, here are a few recommendations:

- Upgrade to MS-DOS 5 or 6 or to DR DOS so you can take advantage of the memory management commands (such as HIMEM, HIDOS, LOADHIGH, DEVICEHIGH, HIDEVICE, and so on) discussed in prior lessons.

- Determine the amount of memory that can be added to the system board (motherboard); you may need to purchase a memory board in order to add memory.

- If you plan to run Windows or other programs (such as a RAM disk or disk cache) which use extended memory, add extended memory as needed. If your present system came with 1MB of RAM, you have only 384K of extended memory!

- If you plan to run programs that use expanded memory (such as Lotus 1-2-3), add expanded memory through an EMS card. Make sure that the card is compatible with the LIM 4.0 standard. Also, if your system does not come with the total 640K of conventional memory, you can backfill (fill in) the missing memory through an option on your expanded memory card.

- You may want to purchase a third-party memory manager such as QRAM or 386MAX version 6.x (386MAX includes a program called MOVE'EM, which is designed for 8088/8086/80286 PCs, and used to be sold separately), to create UMBs for loading DOS, device drivers, and TSRs.

- Consider replacing the system board (motherboard) to upgrade to a 386 or 486 CPU. In some cases it might be inexpensive, but you'll have a faster PC to boot!

If You Own a 386 PC (or Above) and Don't Use Windows

If you own a PC with a 386 CPU or above, but don't plan to use Microsoft Windows, there are many memory management options available. Here are a few recommendations:

- Upgrade to DOS 5, DOS 6, or DR DOS so you can take advantage of the memory management commands (such as HIMEM, EMM386, LOADHIGH, DEVICEHIGH, HIDEVICE, and so on) discussed in prior lessons.

- If you use DOS 6, you can utilize the new memory management utility called MemMaker, which analyzes your software and hardware and then sets up your computer's memory in the most efficient way it can. Other third-party memory management utility vendors sell DOS loaders, but the one that comes with DOS 6 is effectively "free." Check out Lesson 22 for more on the DOS 6 utility called MemMaker.

- If you plan to run programs that use expanded memory (such as Lotus 1-2-3), simulate expanded memory with extended memory through EMM386. Do not add an expanded memory board for this purpose; it will be significantly slower.

- Create UMBs with DOS=UMB for loading DOS, device drivers, and TSRs.

- Set FILES to 20 and BUFFERS to 30, and then adjust as needed.

- If you have additional memory to play around with, consider creating either a RAM disk, or a disk cache.

If You Own a 386 PC (or Above) and Use Windows

If you own a PC with a 386 CPU or above, and plan to use Microsoft Windows, there are many memory management options available. Here are a few recommendations:

- Upgrade to DOS 5, DOS 6, or DR DOS so you can take advantage of the memory management commands (such as HIMEM, EMM386, LOADHIGH, DEVICEHIGH, HIDEVICE, and so on) discussed in prior lessons.

- If you use DR DOS, make the appropriate changes to the CONFIG.SYS and AUTOEXEC.BAT files (see Lesson 17).

- Windows uses extended memory, so add extended memory as needed. A good starting point is 4MB.

- Even if you plan to run programs that use expanded memory (such as Lotus 1-2-3), do not specify any expanded memory through EMM386. Windows simulates whatever is needed when that program is running. Include the NOEMS parameter with the EMM386 command.

- Create UMBs with DOS=UMB for loading DOS, device drivers, and TSRs. Avoid loading anything into conventional memory, especially if you plan to use DOS applications with Windows.

- Set FILES to 20 and BUFFERS to 30 if you are not using SMARTDRV, and set FILES to 20 and BUFFERS to 3 if you are. Adjust as needed.

- If you have additional unused memory, consider creating either a RAM disk (virtual memory) or a disk cache.

If Your PC Is on a Network

Whether your PC has a hard drive or not, it benefits from additional memory to reduce transactions through the network:

- Upgrade to DOS 5, DOS 6, or DR DOS so you can take advantage of the memory management commands (such as HIMEM, EMM386, LOADHIGH, DEVICEHIGH, HIDEVICE, and so on) discussed in prior lessons.

- Create UMBs for loading the network driver, along with DOS, device drivers, and TSRs. Network drivers can take up precious conventional memory.

- Add additional extended memory, as needed, to create a large RAM disk (from 2 to 4MB) for holding programs locally in your RAM. This reduces the number of requests going over the network.

In this lesson, you learned specific strategies that you can apply to your PC. In the next lesson, you will learn important information that you should know if you are planning to upgrade the memory on your PC.

Lesson 21
What to Shop for When Upgrading Memory

In this lesson, you'll learn about the different kinds of memory chips and how to choose appropriate ones for your system.

Looking at Memory Chips

RAM comes in two different types: *dynamic* RAM (*DRAMs*) and *static* RAM (*SRAMs*). DRAMs are the most common type. They hold a charge which is interpreted as a 1 or a 0. DRAMs must be periodically recharged to hold their data. This periodic recharging slows down the speed of the DRAM chips and determines how quickly they can be read by the CPU.

SRAMs, on the other hand, do not need to be recharged, so they are faster. SRAMs are also more expensive. If your PC comes with RAM cache, it is probably made up of SRAM chips.

Looking at Chip Packs

RAM chips come packaged in several ways. The most popular type of RAM chip is the DIP, or Dual Inline

Package (see Figure 21.1). The DIP chip looks like a tiny bug with legs which are inserted into sockets which form the connection between the RAM chip and the system.

SIP

DIP

SIMM

Figure 21.1   RAM chips come in many packages.

Another popular RAM chip is the SIMM, or Single Inline Memory Module, also shown in Figure 21.1. The SIMM is a small circuit board which holds several chips. The SIMM makes its connection to the system through gold strips along one edge.

A chip that is similar to the SIMM is the SIP, or Single Inline Package. A SIP looks like a thin chip, with legs on one side. SIPs connect to the system through sockets in much the same way as DIPs.

Factors That Affect Speed

There are three factors that affect the speed in which RAM works: access time, wait state, and interleaving.

The *access time* of a memory chip is the time it takes that chip to locate the data that the CPU wants and to prepare it to be read. As a comparison, suppose you wanted to retrieve a soft drink during a commercial. The amount of time it takes for you to find the soft drink in the refrigerator would be called your *access time*. The access time of the memory chips in your computer is measured in *nanoseconds (ns)*, which is equivalent to 1 billionth of a second. If a memory chip is rated at 80 ns, it is faster than a chip rated at 120 ns. Use this simple rule: look for chips with low access ratings.

Access Time   The amount of time it takes a RAM chip to locate (access) one bit of data.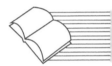

After a RAM chip has been accessed, that address in memory is then read or written to. (In our soft drink analogy, think of this period as the time it takes to open and drain the soft drink can.) After the read/write period, an amount of time must pass in order for the RAM chips to *refresh*. Refreshing is simply recharging; remember that each RAM chip holds (or doesn't hold) a charge that translates in binary as a 1 or a 0. These 1s and 0s form the basis for each character stored in memory.

While a RAM chip goes through its refresh cycle, the CPU gets ready to store another bit. If both the memory chip and the CPU are ready at the same time, there is no waiting; the CPU transfers the number to the RAM chip and the process starts again. If the CPU is ready to store a number, but the RAM chip has not yet refreshed, the CPU must wait.

The amount of time that the CPU must wait is at least a single clock cycle. Think of the clock as a great metronome; it keeps pace for the CPU. The CPU works on the "downbeat," and each downbeat signals the beginning of another clock cycle. Each clock cycle that the CPU waits while the RAM chip refreshes is called a *wait state*. Zero wait states is the ideal, which means that the CPU is never kept waiting.

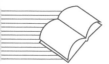 **Wait State**   The number of clock cycles that the CPU must wait while a RAM chip refreshes itself (stores a number and prepares to store another).

RAM chips are arranged on the system board in rows and columns. Each memory address is usually assigned sequentially, such as 010010, 010011, and so on. With *interleaved memory*, memory is divided into two regions— one region is assigned even-numbered memory addresses, the other is assigned odd-numbered ones. Why would this arrangement increase memory speed? Because most programs request data located in sequential addresses. With interleaved memory, while the even address is refreshing, the odd address is ready to be read, and vice versa. The CPU does not have to wait for the memory to refresh; the next memory address to be read is most likely ready.

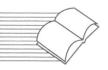 **Interleaved Memory**   A process which speeds memory access by dividing memory into odd- and even-numbered memory addresses.

Choosing the Right Memory Chips for Your System

In order to make sure you purchase the correct type of RAM chip for your system, you need to look at several factors:

- The capacity of the chip, which is usually shown as 64 (as in 64K), 256 (256K) or 1,100 (1MB).

- The speed (access time) of the chip, which is rated in nanoseconds. The speed of the chip appears after the capacity, such as 60. Check your PC manual to determine the optimum speed for chips in your system.

- The capacity of the chips your system takes. Some systems require upgrades of certain amounts. Check your PC manual to be sure how your system can be configured.

- The type of chip your system uses. Does it use DIP, SIMM, or SIP chips?

- The number of chips you need. Remember that nine chips are needed to complete a bank of memory. Therefore, if you needed 512K of RAM, and you were going to use 256K chips, you would need 18 of them, or two banks. Each bank would be "worth" 256K.

Don't Forget to Run Setup When you add memory to a 286, 386, or 486 PC, you often need to run your PC's setup program to tell your system that you have added additional memory.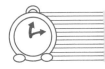

In this lesson, you learned how to choose the right memory chips for your system if you should choose to upgrade. In the next lesson, you will learn about additional memory management software (called third-party programs).

Lesson 22
MemMaker and Third-Party Products

In this lesson, you will learn about DOS 6's MemMaker utility, a DOS program that will set up your system's memory management program for you. We'll also learn about some popular third-party memory management software products.

MS-DOS 6's MemMaker

MS-DOS version 6 comes with several of the same memory management tools as DOS 5, including HIMEM.SYS and EMM386.EXE. The big news with the coming of DOS 6 is the addition of a true *DOS Loader*. A DOS Loader is a program that analyzes your hardware and software and then configures your PC for optimum management of its memory. If you're a little shy about editing your own AUTOEXEC.BAT and CONFIG.SYS files to configure your computer's memory, try using MemMaker instead of trudging through all the procedures in earlier lessons.

MemMaker actually interviews you to determine the type of work done with the computer, then it configures your CONFIG.SYS and AUTOEXEC.BAT files for optimum performance. It can analyze your hardware and software to determine the best "fit" for programs, device drivers, and TSRs that can be loaded into upper memory.

Network Users . . . If you're part of a network, log on before running MemMaker.

To run MEMMAKER:

1. Type MEMMAKER.

2. Press Enter.

You'll be asked to choose between two methods: Express and Custom. Express Setup makes your choices for you, while Custom Setup prompts you to make informed choices as MemMaker does its work. Depending on which method you choose, MemMaker will ask you different questions. Some of the questions you may be called upon to answer include:

- Whether or not you use Windows.

- Whether you use any programs that require expanded memory. If you're not sure, the best "guessing" answer is No.

- Which drivers and TSRs are to be optimized, if not all of them. You opt to include or exclude the drivers and TSRs currently in your startup files one-by-one.

- Whether or not you want to "Scan Aggressively," squeezing every last bit of available memory. This may result in better memory management, but there is a greater chance that MemMaker won't be able to get it right on the first try (that is, your PC may lock up temporarily while it's working).

- Whether you want to use the region of memory reserved for Monochrome display adapters as available memory for programs. You can pick up a little extra memory capacity if you don't *ever* run a monitor in monochrome mode!

141

- Whether you want to keep your current command lines for both EMM386 and HIMEM.

- Whether you want to copy BIOS instructions from conventional memory to the UMA.

MemMaker then comes up with its own idea of the ideal memory-management scenario and reboots your computer, using it's own suggested configuration. As it does so, note any problems as your newly organized device drivers and TSRs load and run.

If there are no problems, you're home free. You quit MemMaker and save the configuration. If any error messages appeared during the booting of the new configuration, you can opt to use your original CONFIG.SYS and AUTOEXEC.BAT files instead of MemMaker's creations.

After MemMaker Does Its Work

Peek at the new configuration to see the tweaking and tailoring that MemMaker did by using the following commands:

```
TYPE CONFIG.SYS
TYPE AUTOEXEC.BAT
```

Depending on the complexity of your boot files, there may be many changes—many of them too technical to be of interest to the average user. Any command line switch and parameter that could be used may be in use. It would take a person many hours to accomplish the same process with any degree of success.

Why Purchase a Different Memory Management Program?

With the improved memory management capabilities of MS-DOS, DR DOS, and DOS 6's MemMaker addition, why would you want to purchase an additional program for managing memory? There are several reasons:

- If you don't have DOS 6, you don't have a DOS Loader program, and you must configure your memory "by hand" as you've learned to do in previous lessons. If you don't want to upgrade to DOS 6 but find using EMM386 or HIDOS cumbersome, a third-party program is made for you.

- Most DOS Loaders can determine the best order for loading TSRs and device drivers into upper memory to take advantage of more UMB space. MemMaker does this, but other programs do so more aggressively.

- You may not own a 386 or 486 PC. Although DR DOS does provide limited support for 286s, MS-DOS does not, even in version 6. However, there are many good memory management programs you can purchase for 286 PCs.

- Although DOS can load some of itself into upper memory, there are parts that it can't load there. Some third-party memory management programs can load *all* of DOS's data structures (not just BUFFERS, but FILES, FCBS, and LASTDRIVE) into upper memory.

A Look at QEMM-386

QEMM-386 is a memory management program from Quarterdeck Office Systems, designed to run on 386 and 486

143

PCs. QEMM-386 version 6.0 comes with an impressive array of features:

- QEMM-386 employs a new technology called Stealth, which can find ROM areas in upper memory that are not really being used by your system, and turn them into UMBs. Stealth technology dramatically increases the amount of UMB space available on your system.

- Through a program called Optimize, QEMM-386 is capable of determining the best order for loading TSRs and device drivers into upper memory. This strategy takes advantage of more UMB space than does EMM386 or HIDOS.

- One program, QEMM386.SYS, replaces both EMM386.EXE and HIMEM.SYS with its capability to manage upper memory, extended memory, and expanded memory.

- Through its DOS Resource Programs, QEMM-386 can load all of the DOS data structures (FILES, BUFFERS, FCBS, and LASTDRIVE) into upper memory. EMM386 can only load BUFFERS.

- QEMM-386 includes a program called Manifest, which is one of the best utility programs available for determining your PC's memory usage. Manifest goes well beyond the MEM command.

- QEMM-386 is compatible with Windows.

- QEMM-386 pools all available memory, creating expanded memory out of extended memory "on the fly," when programs need it. This makes maximum use of both extended and expanded memory.

- Using a program called VIDRAM, QEMM-386 fools DOS into using the first area of upper memory as conventional memory. The amount of conventional memory that DOS thinks is available increases by 96K. This area of upper memory is normally used for the CGA and VGA video RAM. If you only run programs in text mode (no graphics), this feature is a nice one for you.

- A program called Squeeze provides smooth installation of all TSRs and device drivers. Some programs require more memory during their loading phase than they do to actually run. With DOS, these areas of upper memory go unused after programs have been initialized. But not with Squeeze. Squeeze allows a program to "shrink" after its initialization, freeing more upper memory.

Using Manifest, QEMM's Memory Analysis Tool

Manifest is a top-flight memory analysis tool, as shown in Figure 22.1. Manifest provides you with a comprehensive view of your PC's memory: how it's being used, where unused memory can be found, and recommendations for improving efficiency. Manifest comes with a handy print feature for making a permanent copy of its findings.

Manifest analyzes these areas:

- **System** Listings include the type of CPU, the BIOS version (and BIOS date), the amount and type of memory present, and the amount of memory available for use. The System option can also display the contents of your PC's CONFIG.SYS and AUTOEXEC.BAT files. In addition, the System option can be used to display and save CMOS information.

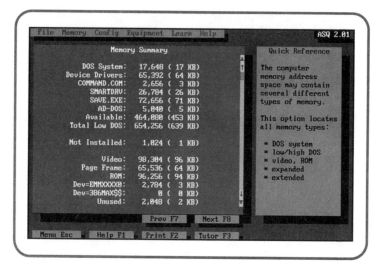

Figure 22.1 Manifest places vital memory management information at your fingertips.

- **First Meg** Listings include the size and location of programs and operating files located in the first MB, a listing of program service interrupts, the contents of the BIOS Data Area, and the memory access times.

- **Expanded Memory** Listings include the type and amount of expanded memory, the location of the expanded memory page frame, and the expanded memory benchmark tests (speed comparisons).

- **Extended Memory** Listings include the amount of expanded memory present and in use, the amount of high memory available, and the amount of upper memory available.

- **DOS** Listings include the amount of memory in use by DOS and its programs, the amount and type of each DOS resource (FILES, BUFFERS, FCBS,

LASTDRIVE, STACKS, and device drivers), and the contents of the DOS environment.

- **QEMM-386**   Listings include QEMM-386's status, its view of memory, its recommendations, and its memory allocations.

- **DESQview**   Listings include DESQview version and memory status.

A Look at QRAM

QRAM is a memory management program from Quarterdeck Office Systems designed for 80286 and 8086/8088 PCs with expanded memory or special chip sets. QRAM allows you to:

- Create UMBs with its upper memory manager.

- Load TSRs and device drivers into upper memory.

- Load DOS resources into upper memory.

- Fool DOS into using the first area of upper memory as conventional memory, with the same VIDRAM program included with QEMM-386.

A Look at 386MAX and BlueMAX

The 386MAX and the BlueMAX are memory management programs by Qualitas. The 386MAX is designed to be used on 386/486 PCs, and the BlueMAX is designed for IBM PS/2s only.

147

Something for Everyone 386MAX version 6.x now includes MOVE'EM, a memory management package for 8088/8086 PCs (with EMS memory) and 80286 PCs. MOVE'EM used to be sold separately, but with its inclusion, 386MAX can be used on all types of PCs.

Both 386MAX and BlueMAX provide the capability to:

- Find ROM areas in upper memory that are not really being used by your system, and turn them into UMBs.

- Convert extended memory into expanded memory.

- Provide smooth installation of all TSRs and device drivers through its FlexFrame technology. Some programs require more memory during their loading phase than they do to actually run. With DOS, these areas of upper memory go unused after programs have been initialized. But not with Squeeze. Squeeze allows a program to "shrink" after its initialization, freeing more upper memory.

- Determine your PC's memory usage with a program called ASQ. ASQ goes well beyond the MEM command, as shown in Figure 22.2.

- Create a RAM disk or a disk cache.

- Fool DOS into using the first area of upper memory as conventional memory. The amount of conventional memory that DOS thinks is available increases by 96K. This area of upper memory is normally used for the CGA and VGA video RAM. If you only run programs in text mode (no graphics), this feature is a nice one for you.

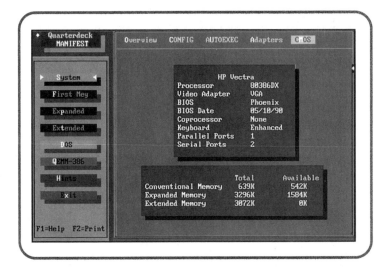

Figure 22.2 ASQ is a memory management tool provided with 386MAX and BlueMAX.

- Load TSRs and device drivers into upper memory in the best order. This strategy takes advantage of more UMB space than EMM386 or HIDOS.

- Create expanded memory out of extended memory "on the fly," when programs need it. This makes maximum use of both extended and expanded memory.

- Improve the performance of Windows.

MOVE'EM, which is included with 386MAX version 6.x, can be used on 286 PCs and 8088/8086 PCs with expanded memory that is compatible with the EMS 4.0 standard. MOVE'EM can be used to provide access to upper memory.

This concludes the *10 Minute Guide to Memory Management*. You have learned all the basics you need to make the most of your PC's memory. Following this lesson is a glossary of memory management terms that will help reinforce your new skills.

149

Glossary

640K Barrier See *DOS barrier*.

A20 Handler Enables 286, 386, and 486 CPUs to access high memory.

Access Time The amount of time it takes a RAM chip to locate (access) one bit of data.

ANSI.SYS A DOS device driver used to enhance the capabilities of a PC's keyboard and monitor.

AUTOEXEC.BAT A special file that *automatically executes* commands when you start your system.

Bit (Binary Digit) A bit is one eighth of a byte, represented by either a positive or negative (*on* or *off*) electronic charge.

Boot Diskette A diskette that you create, which is used to start your PC if you have trouble booting from the hard drive.

Boot Drive Usually drive C, the drive containing your AUTOEXEC.BAT, CONFIG.SYS, and COMMAND.COM files.

Booting The process of starting a PC. You can *boot* your machine two ways. The first is a *cold* or *hard* boot, performed by pressing your computer's reset button or powering-down (and then restarting) the computer. The *soft* or *warm* boot is performed by holding down the Ctrl+Alt+Delete keys at the same time.

BUFFERS A statement placed in the CONFIG.SYS which sets the number of disk buffers.

Byte   A group of 8 bits that represent a character, such as the letter F or the number 101.

Central Processing Unit   A small microchip which acts as the brain of your computer.

CHKDSK   A DOS command (available on all DOS versions) that displays available memory in a manner similar to MEM.

CMOS RAM   Also known as Complimentary Metal-Oxide Semiconductor RAM. CMOS RAM stores basic information about your computer, such as the amount of memory, the type of monitor, the size and type of each drive, and the PC's internal clock.

CONFIG.SYS   A file which is used to customize DOS by loading special device drivers for optional PC equipment, or to change DOS system parameters, such as FILES, BUFFERS, and so on.

Conventional Memory   Also known as lower memory. This is the area of memory (0K to 640K) in which your programs run.

CPU   See *Central Processing Unit.*

DEVICE   A DOS command that, when used in the CONFIG.SYS file, loads a device driver into *lower* memory.

Device Drivers   Special programs that supplement the DOS BIOS by providing instructions for interfacing with optional hardware such as a mouse, a tape drive backup system, a network interface, and so on.

DEVICEHIGH   An MS-DOS command which is used to load device drivers into *upper* memory.

DIP   Also known as Dual Inline Package. A common type of RAM chip which looks like a tiny bug with legs which are inserted into sockets on the system board.

Disk Buffers   An area in RAM where information going to or from a disk is placed temporarily. The buffers are scanned prior to seeking that same data on the disk. Disk buffers work like a disk cache, but they are less intuitive, so they are not as fast as disk caches.

Disk Cache   Pronounced *cash*, a disk cache works like a disk buffer, but it is more intelligent. A disk cache is able to better determine which data is used most often, and therefore should be kept in the cache. There are also RAM caches.

Disk Operating System   Also known as DOS. The Disk Operating System manages basic system functions such as reading a disk, saving a file, or managing the use of memory.

Diskette Drive   Reads removable diskettes that you place in its slot. Like the hard drive, diskettes store data, although in smaller amounts.

DOS   See *Disk Operating System.*

DOS Barrier   Also known as the 640K barrier. The arbitrary division between conventional (program) memory (0K to 640K) and upper (system) memory (640K to 1MB).

DOS Command   An MS-DOS command used to load DOS into high memory. This command can also be used to load device drivers and TSRs into upper memory.

DRAMs   Also known as dynamic RAM. DRAMs must be periodically recharged to hold their data. This periodic recharging slows down the speed of the DRAM chips.

EMM386.EXE   An MS-DOS device driver that provides access to extended memory, fills UMBs with memory so that device drivers and TSRs can be loaded there, and simulates expanded memory with extended memory.

EMS   See Expanded Memory Specification.

Enhanced Mode   A Windows operating mode (for 386 PCs and above) that uses conventional and extended memory. Any existing expanded memory is ignored by Windows.

Expanded Memory   Special memory that's accessed through a page frame in upper memory. The page frame swaps memory back and forth between upper memory and expanded memory.

Expanded Memory Specification   Abbreviated EMS. The standards for accessing expanded memory.

Expansion Boards   Circuit boards which can be added to your system expanding the capability of your computer. For example, expansion boards can be used to add additional memory.

Extended Memory   The area of RAM above the 1MB mark. Extended memory can be used for data storage by programs that are designed for it. Extended memory can be made to simulate expanded memory.

Extended Memory Specification   Abbreviated XMS. The standards for accessing extended memory.

File Handles   Used by programs to track open files. Each file handle uses from 40 to 60 bytes of RAM. Most programs will specify the number of file handles that they need.

FILES   A statement placed in the CONFIG.SYS which limits the number of file handles (indexes which track open files).

Formatting   The process of preparing a diskette for use.

Hard Drive   Also known as hard disk. A permanent storage area located inside the computer, where you store programs and data files.

Hidden Files   Special files which supplement the ROM BIOS. These files reside on your boot drive, but they cannot be displayed with the DIR command.

High Memory Area   Also known as HMA. Located in the first 64K of extended memory, the HMA is only available on PCs with a 286 microprocessor (and above).

HIMEM.SYS   An MS-DOS device driver used to provide access to the high memory area.

INSTALL   A DOS command that loads programs named in your CONFIG.SYS file without creating additional *environment* space for that program. Some programs don't require environment space, so some system memory can be saved by using the INSTALL command in certain cases.

Interleaved Memory   Memory is divided into two regions—even and odd memory addresses. While an even address is refreshing, the odd address is ready to be read, and vice versa. The CPU does not have to wait for the memory to refresh because the next memory address to be read is most likely ready.

Interrupts   Interrupts are a means for some hardware component (such as a keyboard or a mouse) to get the CPU to do something, such as open a file, read a diskette, or record keypresses. When an interrupt occurs, the CPU will stop what it is doing to attend to it.

Kernel   The kernel is the part of DOS that acts as the manager of your PC. The kernel handles the job of receiving requests and delegating tasks.

Kilobyte   A unit of measure equal to approximately 1,000 bytes (really it's 1,024 bytes).

LOADHIGH   An MS-DOS command that is used to load TSRs (and certain device drivers) into upper memory.

Local Area Network (LAN)   See *network*.

Lost Clusters   A lost cluster or chain is caused when DOS does not update its file listing properly. When you delete a file, that file is not erased; only the file reference (the file's name and location on disk) is erased. If the name of the file is erased from the file listing, but the address is still marked occupied, you get a lost cluster.

Lower Memory   See *conventional memory*.

Megabyte   A unit of measure equal to approximately 1,000,000 bytes (really it's 1,024K or 1,048,576 bytes).

MEM   A DOS command (available on DOS 4.0 and above) that is used to determine your PC's memory configuration.

MemMaker   A DOS 6 utility that automatically sets up your startup files to manage your memory.

Memory   Memory is a place where information is stored on microchips. The two types of memory are RAM and ROM.

Motherboard   See *System Board.*

Nanoseconds   Abbreviated (ns), one nanosecond is equivalent to 1 billionth of a second. RAM chips with lower ratings (80 ns versus 120 ns) are faster.

Network   Also known as LAN or Local Area Network. A network is a group of computers and computer equipment connected through cables. Data and equipment can be shared through a network.

Page Frame   An unused area of upper memory which forms the gateway to expanded memory. Data is copied from expanded memory into the page frame for processing, and then back out again.

PATH   A statement in the AUTOEXEC.BAT that provides DOS with a list of directories to search for when program files are not located in the current directory.

Power On Self Test   Also known as POST. This test occurs at boot, checking your PC's equipment and each RAM chip.

Printer Buffer   A temporary storage area where printer data is transferred and held until the printer can print it. In this manner, a PC can continue working as the printer continues to print.

PROMPT   A command placed in the AUTOEXEC.BAT used to customize the DOS prompt. A common variation of the PROMPT command is `PROMPT $P$G`.

Protected Mode   In order to address memory areas above 1MB, the CPU must be switched to protected mode. These additional addresses are accessed with the help of the extended memory manager.

RAM   See *Random Access Memory.*

RAM Cache   A RAM cache is made of faster RAM chips (usually SRAMs) which hold copies of some of the data in regular RAM. The CPU checks the RAM cache for requested data, and if it is there, that data is accessed more quickly than from regular RAM. There are also disk caches.

RAM Disk   A disk drive created in memory. A RAM disk looks and acts like any other disk drive (such as C:). Information can be quickly read and written to it because it is made out of memory. However, because a RAM disk is made of memory, its data is erased when the PC is turned off.

RAMDRIVE.SYS   An MS-DOS device driver that comes with DOS 5; prior versions used VDISK.SYS. RAMDRIVE can be used to create a RAM disk in either conventional, expanded, or extended memory.

Random Access Memory   Also known as RAM. RAM is the working area of the computer, providing temporary storage of information. Information is calculated, changed, and otherwise manipulated in RAM.

Read Only Memory   Also known as ROM. ROM contains permanent information about the basic operations of your computer, such as how to read a diskette, store a file, and open a file. Information contained in ROM can't be changed because ROM can be read, but not written to.

Real Mode   The CPU's normal operating mode. In real mode, only memory addresses up to 1MB can be accessed by the CPU.

ROM   See *Read Only Memory*.

SET   A statement placed in the AUTOEXEC.BAT used to place notes into the environment area for your programs.

Shadow RAM   Lets your PC run faster by copying the ROM information into RAM. When basic input/output instructions are needed, those instructions are read from RAM, which is faster than trying to read them from ROM.

SHELL   A statement placed in the CONFIG.SYS which lets you specify where COMMAND.COM is located on your boot disk, or to increase the environment space.

SIMM   See *Single Inline Memory Module*.

Single Inline Memory Module   Also known as SIMM. The SIMM is a small circuit board which holds several RAM chips. The SIMM makes its connection to the system through gold strips along one edge.

Single Inline Package   Also known as SIP. A SIP is a thin chip, with legs on one side. SIPs connect to the system through sockets in the same way as DIPs.

SIP   See *Single Inline Package*.

SMARTDRV.SYS   An MS-DOS device driver used to create a disk cache.

SRAMs   Also known as static RAM. SRAMs do not need to be recharged, so they are faster than DRAM chips. If your PC comes with a RAM cache, it is probably made up of SRAM chips.

STACKS   A statement placed in the CONFIG.SYS limiting the stack area in memory. which keeps track of interrupts.

Standard Mode   A Windows operating mode using conventional memory and extended memory only. In standard mode, existing expanded memory is ignored by Windows as it acts as an intermediary between DOS and the application, passing the requests for expanded memory to DOS.

Static RAM   See *SRAMs*.

Switch   A character or word following the name of a DOS command or file that applies direction to that command or file's execution.

System Board   Known also as the *motherboard*. Located on the floor of the system unit, the system board connects the various electronic pieces of your PC.

System Memory   See *upper memory*.

Terminate and Stay Resident   See *TSR*.

Text File   Files that don't include special effects, such as bold or italic. The CONFIG.SYS and the AUTOEXEC.BAT are text files.

TSR   Also known as Terminate and Stay Resident programs. These utility programs go to sleep after they start, and they are reactivated when you want them. You use TSRs with other programs; for example, you could activate a TSR while you are in your word processor to add a column of figures, or to change an appointment.

UMB Also known as Upper Memory Blocks. Areas of upper memory which normally go unused. Through the use of an upper memory device driver, you can utilize this seldom used area of memory.

Upper Memory Also known as *adapter memory*. Upper memory (640K to 1M) was designed for DOS and your computer hardware's use, but can be used for TSRs and device drivers.

VDISK.SYS A DR DOS and MS-DOS (versions prior to DOS 5) device driver. VDISK can be used to create a RAM disk in either conventional, expanded, or extended memory.

Video RAM Lets complex video graphics quickly appear on your computer's monitor. Video RAM is dedicated to the task of holding data which is moved between your video card and your CPU. Also known as VRAM.

Virtual Memory Additional memory capacity that's simulated by using hard disk space.

Wait State The number of clock cycles that the CPU must wait while a RAM chip refreshes itself (stores a number and prepares to store another). Zero wait states is the ideal, which means that the CPU is never kept waiting.

Write-Protect Write-protecting a diskette prevents data on the diskette from being changed or deleted.

Index

DOS barrier, 8-11, 152
DOS BIOS routines, 10
DOS command, 152
  DOS=HIGH, 56, 77-79
  DOS=UMB, 58
DOS Loaders, 140
DOS prompt, customizing, 43
double-buffering, 120-121
DR DOS, 53-54
  disk caches, 122-123
  EDITOR text editor, 83-86
  EMM386.SYS device driver,
    91-95
  EMMXMA.SYS device driver,
    95-96
  extended memory, 59-60
  HIDOS.SYS device driver,
    88-91
  kernel, moving to high/upper
    memory, 91-95
  loading
    device drivers into upper
      memory, 58, 99-100
  · DOS data structures into
      upper memory, 97-98
    HMA (high memory area), 56
    TSRs into upper memory, 58,
      101-103
  VDISK program, 127-128
  with Windows, 116-117
DRAMs, 135, 152

E

EDIT text editor, 61-66
EDITOR text editor, 83-86
EMM386.EXE device driver,
  72-76, 152
EMM386.SYS device driver, 54,
  91-95
EMMXMA.SYS device driver,
  60, 95-96

EMS (Expanded Memory
  Specification), 16-18
enhanced mode, 112-114, 152
environment space, increasing,
  38-39
expanded memory, 16-18, 152
  creating with extended memory,
    59-60, 72, 91, 95-96
Expanded Memory Specification
  (EMS), 152
expansion boards, 2, 153
extended memory, 14-16, 153
  creating expanded memory
    with, 59-60, 72, 91, 95-96
  displaying information, 22
  making available, 59, 72-76,
    91-95
extended memory managers,
  14-15
Extended Memory Specification
  (XMS), 14-16, 153

F-G

FCBS (File Control Block
    System) command, 36, 108
files
  control blocks, 36
  DOS operating system,
    copying, 47-48
  EDIT text editor, saving, 66
  handles, 36-37, 153
  hidden, 153
  opening, 64, 84
  saving, 5, 86
  SYS extension, 34
  text, 157
FILES command, 36-37, 108, 153
FlexFrame technology, 148
floppy disks, *see* diskettes
FORMAT command, 47-48
formatting diskettes, 47-52, 153
free memory, displaying amounts,
  28-30

161

H

handles, files, 36-37, 153
hard boots, 150
hard disks, disk caching, 120-122
hard drives, 2, 153
hidden files, 153
HIDEVICE command, 58, 99-100
HIDOS command, 97-98
HIDOS.SYS device driver, 54,
    88-91
high memory
    loading DOS, 77-79
    moving DR DOS kernel, 91-95
high memory area (HMA),
    16, 153
    accessing, 54-55, 68-72, 88-91
    device drivers, 16
    loading, 55-56
HIINSTALL command, 58,
    101-102
HILOAD command, 58, 102-103
HIMEM.SYS device driver,
    54-55, 68-72, 153
Hyperdisk program, 118

I-J

InfoSpotter software, 26
INSTALL command, 153
Interactive Start, 46-47
interleaved memory, 138, 154
interrupts, 37-38, 154

K-L

kernel, 88, 154
    moving to high/upper memory,
        91-95
kilobytes (K), 7, 154

LANs (Local Area Networks), 155
LOADHIGH command, 58,
    81-82, 154

lost clusters, 30, 154
lower memory, *see* conventional
    memory

M

Manifest memory detection
    software, 26, 144-147
mapping UMBs, 57-58
megabytes (M), 7, 154
MEM command, 19-25, 154
MEMMAKER command, 141
MemMaker program,
    140-142, 154
memory, 2-3, 154
    640K barrier, 8-11, 152
    Adapter RAM/ROM, 22
    conventional, 9-10, 151
    determining usage, 145-147
    displaying information about,
        19-26
    expanded, 16-18, 152
        creating with extended
            memory, 59-60, 72, 91,
            95-96
    extended, 14-16, 153
        making available, 59, 72-76,
            91-95
    free, displaying amounts, 28-30
    high, *see* high memory
    high memory area (HMA), 16
        accessing, 54-55, 68-72, 88-91
    interleaved, 138, 154
    RAM, *see* RAM
    ROM, 4
    storage, versus disk storage, 3
    third-party management
        programs, 143-149
    units of measurement, 7
    upper, *see* upper memory
    virtual, 113, 158
Memory Commander, 118, 124
MemoryMAX, 87

T

U

V

W

X-Z